T0323982

# Cambridge Elements ≡

**Elements in New Religious Movements**
Series Editor
Rebecca Moore
*San Diego State University*
Founding Editor
†James R. Lewis
*Wuhan University*

# CHILDREN IN NEW RELIGIOUS MOVEMENTS

## Sanja Nilsson
*Dalarna University*

**CAMBRIDGE**
UNIVERSITY PRESS

Shaftesbury Road, Cambridge CB2 8EA, United Kingdom

One Liberty Plaza, 20th Floor, New York, NY 10006, USA

477 Williamstown Road, Port Melbourne, VIC 3207, Australia

314–321, 3rd Floor, Plot 3, Splendor Forum, Jasola District Centre,
New Delhi – 110025, India

103 Penang Road, #05–06/07, Visioncrest Commercial, Singapore 238467

Cambridge University Press is part of Cambridge University Press & Assessment,
a department of the University of Cambridge.

We share the University's mission to contribute to society through the pursuit of
education, learning and research at the highest international levels of excellence.

www.cambridge.org
Information on this title: www.cambridge.org/9781009565127

DOI: 10.1017/9781009067263

© Sanja Nilsson 2024

This publication is in copyright. Subject to statutory exception and to the provisions
of relevant collective licensing agreements, no reproduction of any part may take
place without the written permission of Cambridge University Press & Assessment.

When citing this work, please include a reference to the DOI 10.1017/9781009067263

First published 2024

*A catalogue record for this publication is available from the British Library.*

ISBN 978-1-009-56512-7 Hardback
ISBN 978-1-009-06596-2 Paperback
ISSN 2635-232X (online)
ISSN 2635-2311 (print)

Cambridge University Press & Assessment has no responsibility for the persistence
or accuracy of URLs for external or third-party internet websites referred to in this
publication and does not guarantee that any content on such websites is, or will
remain, accurate or appropriate.

# Children in New Religious Movements

Elements in New Religious Movements

DOI: 10.1017/9781009067263
First published online: November 2024

Sanja Nilsson
*Dalarna University*

**Author for correspondence:** Sanja Nilsson, sns@du.se

**Abstract:** New religious movements have not only arisen in the present but have also developed in the past. While they differ in ideology and practice, they generally seem to live in high tension with mainstream society, especially when it comes to child-rearing. This Element examines several aspects of children growing up in new religions. It relies upon literature from different groups concerning child upbringing, the function of children in the groups considering the religious ideologies, and parental perspectives and parental styles. It also utilizes accounts from young adults growing up in these groups, both those who chose to stay and who chose to leave their groups as adults. A range of topics, such as socialization, education, healthcare, and relations to surrounding society are explored. In addition, this Element considers issues of physical and emotional abuse, state interventions, and the impact of second- and third-generations of children in new religions.

**Keywords:** new religious movements, childhood, religious socialization, religious education, child abuse

ISBNs: 9781009565127 (HB), 9781009065962 (PB), 9781009067263 (OC)
ISSNs: 2635-232X (online), 2635-2311 (print)

# Contents

## 1 Researching Children in New Religious Movements

In November 2019, a total of six minors were removed from the Qahal Yahweh Assembly of St. James, Jamaica after a raid by law-enforcement authorities warranted by allegations of child abuse, child marriage, sexual assault, abduction, and human trafficking. Prompting the raid were allegations from the leader Omar Thompson's former wife and mother of his three children, who were among those taken into custody. Four years later, in June 2023, the group's communal living quarters were again raided, and this time twenty-one children were taken into custody, with charges of neglect due to not vaccinating the children. All twenty-one children were released in November 2023; however, thirteen members of the congregation will stand trial accused of violation of the Child Care and Protection Act in February 2024. Media reports include child protection advocates stating that deeper knowledge into the group's beliefs and practices are needed.

Similar cases of reported child abuse in what is to the public known as "religious cults" has become a recurring theme in the news. The interest in religious groups that deviate from the mainstream paired with an increasing focus on children's rights has become an important part of popular culture. Through documentaries and podcasts portraying life in the group, most often through the eyes of defectors: the public is sometimes with those who spent their childhoods in such a group. Rarely do we hear from children while they are children, and rarer still, while they are in the congregation of their parents' choice. The controversies surrounding the new religions, or cults, have shifted focus from claims of brainwashed adult members in the 1970s to the current focus on indoctrination (and sometimes abuse) of children in said groups. This Element explores the current academic field of research relating to children in new religions and regards various aspects of socialization, education, healthcare, and relations to surrounding society. Additionally, it considers issues of physical and emotional abuse, state interventions, and the impact of second- and third-generations of children in new religions.

The academic study of children growing up in new religions is a fairly young and unexplored research field. Scholars involved in the study come from different disciplines, such as sociology, psychology, child and youth studies, and social work. Within the sociology of religion, childhood in these groups has generally been studied as a part of one particular group presented as a section in a monograph as, for instance, in Kenneth Wooden's book *The Children of Jonestown* (1981), James Chancellor's book *Life in the Family* on The Family International, formerly Children of God (2000), and E. Burke Rochford's *Hare Krishna Transformed* on ISKCON (2007). Although comprehensive studies on childhood in new religious movements are still rare, there is the excellent contemporary work of Susan Palmer and Charlotte Hardman in their anthology *Children in New Religions* (1999), Amanda van Eck Duymaer van Twist's *Perfect Children* (2015), and Janja Lalich and Karla McLaren's *Escaping Utopia* (2018). Together with prominent new religion scholars Liselotte Frisk and Peter Åkerbäck, I cowrote the anthology *Children in Minority Religions* (2018), which covers some of the new religions' history regarding children and childhood in Sweden. My book *Kids of Knutby: Living in and Leaving the Swedish Filadelfia Congregation* (2023) analyzed the situation for children and youth growing up in the congregation of the charismatic Christian new religion Knutby Filadelfia in Sweden 2014–2018. Jessica Pratezina's dissertation "New Religion Kids" (2019) also provides a unique insight into the lives of children in new religions. There are a few older works worth mentioning in relation to the field. John Rothchild and Susan Wolf's book *The Children of the Counterculture* (1976) provides valuable general knowledge on the upbringing of children in the counterculture communities of the 1960s and 1970s. Additionally, Daniel Greenberg's survey of 219 intentional communities (including nonreligious) presented in the thesis "Growing Up in Community" (1993) provides interesting comparative data on childhoods in communities in the United States. Furthermore, *Prophet's Daughter: My Life with Elizabeth Claire Prophet inside the Church Universal and Triumphant* (2008) by Erin Prophet is a valuable source of knowledge. Prophet has since published several interesting academic articles on new religions. Of course, there are many important nonacademic biographical contributions that will enhance the researcher's knowledge of the various aspects of experiences of childhoods in new religious movements.

In studies of new religions, the concept of what constitutes a new religion has a history of being debated. As we shall see, the terms *cult* and *sect* have been rejected by large parts of the academic community, as the understanding of the terms has switched from being used as a purely sociological term to connoting "bad," "false," or "dangerous" religion in the public use of the words, not least by sensationalistic media. Due to this development, the term new religious movements came to be employed (Lewis & Petersen, 2005). Additionally, some scholars differentiate between *old* and *new* new religious movements. Four prominent and still active old new religions from the nineteenth century are the Church of Jesus Christ of Latter-day Saints, the Church of Christ, Scientist, the Plymouth Brethren Christian Church, and the Jehovah's Witnesses (Lewis & Tøllefsen, 2016). Newer new religions are typically categorized as groups that came into existence after World War II, such as the Church of Scientology, Hare Krishna (ISKCON), Trancendental Meditation,

The Family International (because the group is known both as the Children of God and The Family International, henceforward it will be identified as COG/TFI), and many more. Additionally, scholars of new religions normally differentiate between the *organized* new religious *movements* and the less organized New Age *milieu* (see, e.g., Løøv, 2024). The latter is harder to demarcate and because of the sometimes-derogatory connotation of the concept of New Age, scholars also use New Spirituality or New Religion. An interesting development pertaining to this milieu regarding children and childhoods is the emergence of spiritually based ideas about the so-called Indigo and Crystal Children. In this Element, I will use the term new religious movements. The debate over the use of cults or new religions is centered on the notion that a cult may be totalitarian or sectarian. However, the term new religious movements allows a broader understanding and aims at avoiding the connotations of violence that the word cult has. My position is that a new religious movement exhibits different levels of sectarianism and totalitarianism, and is subject to change, which is why the term new religious movement is preferable as a starting point. However, when referring specifically to other scholars' work, I will simply use the term that the author uses.

Contemporary studies of children in new religions can be traced to the onset of so-called anticult movements of the 1960s and 1970s. When young adults, some merely teenagers, started joining the new movements emerging from the counterculture scene, such as various Jesus People groups and eastern-inspired meditation movements, the older generation, including their parents, were taken aback. These new groups seemed, to them, to devour their young, as they saw their children get swept away in new beliefs and lifestyles, leaving the old ones behind. While confusing to many, some parents were downright upset, scared, and angry. They blamed the groups for their children dropping out of society, deviating from the path staked out by their parents when they were abandoning education and employment in favor of an uncertain communal life with the group of their choice. One group in particular, COG/TFI, caused great anger and concern. Some of the parents of converts to that group founded the first anticult group FREECOG – Free Our Children from the Children of God (Melton, 2002, p. 268). Accusations of mind control and brainwashing followed and eventually former members, who had left other similar groups, joined the ranks of parents and concerned social workers, politicians, therapists, and others opposing the new religious groups.

The controversies surrounding the groups' ways of living, proselytizing, and ideologies, as well as the issue of freedom of religion and cults in general, have been described by Eileen Barker (1984), James A. Beckford (1985), James T. Richardson (2004), Susan Palmer (2011), and several other prominent scholars within the sociology of religion. However, some scholars of psychology adopted what is called brainwashing theory (Singer & Lalich, 1995; Lalich & McLaren, 2018). They argued that sectarian new religious movements manipulated people, converting them against their better judgment. Those who did not adhere to the brainwashing claims still maintained a skeptical and more balanced view of the field, acknowledging that the position of adults and children differed in terms of agency and autonomy. Siskind, for example, argues that

> many social scientists have largely ignored the presence of children in new religious movements, treating these groups as simple voluntary aggregations of consenting adults. Others have recognized the presence of children in these groups but have argued that groups that oppose or retreat from mainstream society are often unfairly persecuted merely because they deviate from the unwritten norms of child-rearing in our society. (Siskind, 2001, p. 434)

Even if most of the converts stayed less than two years in their groups (Barker, 1984), some did, and eventually they had children born into the movements. During the 1980s and 1990s, the focus of cultural opponents and others taking an interest in the groups shifted from brainwashing claims to charges of abuse of children and youth – mostly, but not solely, sexual abuse. Sometimes, physical disciplining of children and youth has provoked criticism from cultural opponents. What constitutes physical abuse against children varies between countries, sometimes resulting in a specific practice prohibited in one country while being legal in another. A recent example of this is the relocation of The Twelve Tribes community in Germany to the Czech Republic. Within the theology of the community, physical discipline of children is imperative to their upbringing, so the practice of spanking children with a short, plastic rod is not negotiable for most parents. Since this constitutes physical abuse in Germany, the German authorities raided the commune in 2013 and placed all the children in state custody.

Custody cases involving children in new religious movements have generally been closely connected to claims of child abuse. One form of cases is those in which one parent left the group and wanted to take the child(ren) with them while the remaining parent opposed this, both arguing that their decision is in the child's best interest in regard to child-rearing practices. It could also involve grandparents seeking legal custody of their grandchildren, claiming that parents' choice to belong to a certain group and adhere to their lifestyle had a negative influence on the child's development or even that it may pose a direct threat to the child's life. In a few cases, the groups tried to separate the children from the nonmember parent, relatives, and authorities, resulting in frequent relocation of the child and accusations of kidnapping. Most often, the decision to hide a child led outsiders to conclude that the parents had given all parental rights to the group, arguably as a result of "brainwashing."

The occurrence of the Jonestown mass murders–suicides in 1978 seemed to support the view that these new religions were dangerous places for children to grow up in. Media's impact on the view of the groups as dangerous cannot be underestimated (Bromley & Shupe, 1987). While there are indeed some groups within which sexual and physical abuse of children did (and does) occur, this was hardly true for all the various groups that kept popping up. However, as some noticeable cases of neglect and abuse came to public knowledge, the situation for the children became the focal point of the criticism against the new religions (Richardson, 1999; Saliba, 2003).

A few of the defectors of the movements left and pursued careers as counselors and therapists, often aiming to help others leaving cope with managing the defection. Coinciding with the Satanic Panic scares of the 1990s (see, for instance, Richardson et al., 1991), the public view of child-rearing in new religions was reduced to a belief in abuse and neglect, and, in the worst case of all, mass murder. To counterbalance this one-sided and erroneous view, sociologists of religion put their research efforts into showing that popular opinion did not necessarily reflect reality. There were indeed large numbers of children who did not suffer neglect or abuse, although they grew up in a very different manner than their peers at school. Because some groups were targeted by cultural opponents more than others, and because of the fact that there was indeed abuse going on in some of the groups, studies of children have tended to focus less on everyday life and more on whether there was abuse or not. Cruelty and mistreatment are naturally imperative to stop, but we also need more research into the everyday lives of the children and youth who grow up in these norm-criticizing environments.

Furthermore, since negative views of the movements have dominated for at least forty years, members of several groups feel stigmatized and falsely accused, simply because they have different views on faith and an unusual lifestyle. Those in a considerable number of groups are painfully aware of the risks of stigma and fear that letting any outsider into their group might cause accusations and lead to negative consequences. This is the main reason that it is difficult to study children in these groups while they are still children. Parents are afraid, and, generally, researching children's religion is beset with rigorous ethical requirements and restrictions, with human subject permits to be obtained. It can take a scholar years to access children within a group. Therefore, most data consist of retrospective life story narratives given by adults who were born and raised in new religious movements. While these are valuable, the current life of the children and youth needs more research.

## 2 Situating the Concept of Childhood

In order to discuss the terms and conditions for children growing up in new religious movements and milieus, we need to start off with the concept of child and childhood itself. This Element presupposes a Western definition of the concept *child* as stated in the United Nations Convention of the Rights of The Child:

> **Article 1** (Definition of the child): The Convention defines a "child" as a person below the age of 18, unless the laws of a particular country set the legal age for adulthood younger. The Committee on the Rights of the Child, the monitoring body for the Convention, has encouraged States to review the age of majority if it is set below 18 and to increase the level of protection for all children under 18. (UNICEF Guiding Principles, 2022)

Childhood is actually a fairly recent invention. French historian Philippe Ariès's widely read book *Centuries of Childhood: A Social History of Family Life* (1962) is understood by many as the first work in modern times in the field of childhood studies (Cunningham, 2005, p. 5). Ariès argues that the concept of childhood did not come into existence until the seventeenth century, as there was no such idea present in the history of medieval Europe. According to Ariès, childhood, as we now understand it, first surfaced in the realm of nuclear family life and in the emergence of the public school system. Prior to that, children were simply understood to be "small adults," a conclusion he draws by studying, among other artifacts of the time, art which shows that there was no difference in children's and adults' clothing (Ariès, 1962, p. 50). As we shall see, the understanding of children as adults in small bodies, or rather, old souls in new bodies, is part of the theology of some of the new religious movements, for example, within the Church of Scientology.

Ariès's work has been severely criticized for being one-sided; nevertheless, it served as a starting point for childhood studies and is still considered a classic within the field. It prompted several books on the subject, for example, Edward Shorter's *The Making of the Modern Family* (1976), Lloyd deMause's *The History of Childhood* (1974), and Lawrence Stone's *The Family, Sex and Marriage in England 1500-1800* (1990). The view that childhood could be studied in its own right was further developed by several historians. Scholars such as Shorter, deMause, and Stone promoted Ariès's argument that there was no separation of children and adults in medieval Europe. Shorter further links the emergence of love-based marriages, as opposed to prearranged, with parental affection. He goes as far as to argue that parents' affection for their children was not visible in society until the arrival of capitalism, which awarded people the choice to marry whomever they wanted. He thus argues that parents lacked affection for their offspring up until the middle of the eighteenth century. DeMause takes this point even further and suggests that the widespread practice of child abuse occurred because parents lacked warm affection for their children. As illustration, he points to practices of swaddling and the use of wet nurses; he further elaborates on the practice of abandoning young children as a manifestation of a society wherein children were not highly regarded. Stone attributes the onset of parental affection with the considerable drop in child mortality rates in the eighteenth century. He claims that this changed the parents' appreciation for each child as an individual who might live to reach adulthood. High mortality rates in medieval Europe were a fact that might have had a negative effect on the attachment between parents and children. However, this analysis disregards the impact of industrialization on other variables, such as hygiene, development of medicine, and proximity to others. Common to all three authors is that they perceive the use of wet nurses and swaddling as evidence for a lack of attachment between children and parents. While swaddling might have gone out of style, the use of other women to care for one's small children within new religions is still uncritically interpreted by outsiders as a lack of affection (and sometimes manipulation).

Linda Pollock challenged the pessimistic view of Shorter, deMause, and Stoner in *Forgotten Children: Parent-Child Relations from 1500 to 1900* (1983). Pollock argues that "there is no correlation between the mortality rates and the supposed developments of affection" (Pollock, 1983, p. 51). She also claims that contrary to deMause in particular, parents *did* care for their children when they were ill, and that parents felt sad when their children died. John Boswell's book *The Kindness of Strangers* (1988) is also a work that contests the view of a dark history of childhood. Boswell suggests that deMause's understanding of child abandonment could be interpreted as an act of care. Children were most often left at the doorstep of a monastery where the parents, unable to provide a good life for them, felt assured they would be well cared for. To leave a child at a monastery could even be seen in terms of religious offering, according to Boswell (1988, p. 229). Boswell's main point, however, is that many children who were abandoned survived by *the kindness of strangers* (Boswell, 1988, p. 44) contrary to deMause's assumption that most of them did not survive (deMause, 1974, p. 34). Historian Shulamith Shahar also writes that parents in the Middle Ages were far more caring of their offspring than was previously thought, which she demonstrates in her book *Childhood in the Middle Ages* (1990).

## Raising Children in Utopian Communes
## of the Nineteenth Century

By the nineteenth century, parental regard for children was taken as normative; thus, controversial religious communities were harshly criticized for experimenting with parental roles. Outsiders viewed communal raising of children as the sign of a lack of parental affection. A few well-known examples inform our understanding of the ways and scope that new views on childhood and child-rearing challenged their contemporary society's assumptions. Moreover, the response from society impacted the existence and practices of the communes. The innovative patterns concerning children and childhood, as well as the emergence of new religious movements, are themselves the result of opposition toward contemporary society. This resistance often includes new beliefs, new ways of life, innovative social organization, sexual experimentation, and rejection of and, to some extent, isolation from society. The very existence of some groups depended upon their oppositional ideas. The Bishop Hill Colony in Illinois (1846–1862), The Oneida Community in New York (1848–1898), and Brook Farm in Massachusetts (1841–1846) are all examples of utopian communes that defied contemporary communities' way of life, understanding of faith, and the societal norms of their time. The construction of childhood, the practical upbringing of children, and the experiences of these children also questioned the contemporary society. There is comprehensive data on these communes, and they operated under the same period in a time of immigration and expansion in the United States (Delano, 2004; Lewis, 2005; Ferrara, 2019).

The Bishop Hill Colony was a utopian religious commune that operated in Illinois between 1846 and 1862. It was founded by the Swedish pietist Erik Janson (1808–1850) who had emigrated from the Swedish village of Biskopskulla (Bishop Hill) situated outside of Uppsala. In Sweden, Janson had become increasingly radicalized, and his preaching had taken on a negative stance against the Swedish Lutheran Church. As a consequence, Janson and his followers were subjected to persecution and left Sweden for America in search of a place to preach and practice in peace. Janson's main theological deviation was his understanding of human beings as sinless, an interpretation rejected by the Swedish Lutheran Church. The so-called Jansonists made up a considerable number – 1400 members followed Janson to Illinois in America to build "The New Jerusalem." The commune persisted for sixteen years. The first child born in the colony was Mary Malmgren (1846–1938). During shorter periods of the commune's existence, especially in times of poverty, celibacy was mandatory. However, after only one year of existence, a school opened in the commune that taught about thirty-five children (Mikelsen, 1892, p. 31). A museum exists on the geographical spot where the group settled (Ferrara, 2019). When the colony – which was more like a small town, including a church, school, hotel, hospital, and successful enterprise – dissolved in 1862, the property was divided between all members over the age of thirty-five. This included men and women alike, something highly unusual at the time (Mikelsen, 1892, p. 67).

The Oneida Community of New York, sometimes referred to as The Oneida Perfectionists, was founded by John Humphrey Noyes (1811–1886) in 1848, and is one of the most researched utopian communes from the nineteenth century. The Oneida community was notorious for Noyes's theology of sexuality, which he called complex marriage – a practice of nonmonogamous relations between adults in the community. Noyes's ideas centered on the communal raising of children, and children had their own living quarters, being cared for by various community members rather than by their biological parents. In this respect, the children's roles in the community were both innovative and provocative for the surrounding society, especially as Noyes himself came to father nine children out of a total of fifty-eight born into the community. A handbook from the community first published in 1867 details the lives of the children, and there are several personal accounts published on the experiences of children in autobiographical form (see, for instance, Noyes, 1937 and 1958, and Robertson, 1981). These show the variety of experiences of growing up in the Oneida community.

The Brook Farm community was founded by Unitarians George (1802–1880) and Sophia (1803–1861) Ripley in Massachusetts in 1841 and existed until 1846. Unlike the other communes, Brook Farm was heavily inspired by American Transcendentalism, a mix of philosophical and religious ideas propagated by Ralph Waldo Emerson (1808–1892). Sophia Ripley managed the community school, which was one of the main sources of income for the community. The school's reputation attracted students from faraway places such as Haiti and the Philippines (Packer, 2007). Its educational system spanned preschool programs to adult education. The pedagogy was progressive in style. Women of the community managed life for the children, although they were not necessarily the biological mothers. This child-centered perspective on education reflects the community's view on childhood, a rather open-minded view at the time.

Experimental aspects of sexual practices and child-rearing are also present in several contemporary new religious movements. Views about children are closely linked to perceptions of womanhood. In some contemporary new religious movements, women are held in high esteem. Consider for instance the Raelian UFO movement that states that women have greater power because they are seen as being more like the Elohim, the extraterrestrial species believed by members to control humanity. An article by Palmer problematizes the role of women in the movement; however, pointing to the myth of creation and the male gender bias in the language of the theology where the father figures repeatedly while the mother is given less attention (Palmer, 1995). Members are mostly discouraged from having children. Should they decide to go ahead anyway, a maximum of two children is recommended, due to the overpopulation of the planet (Palmer, 2004). Another group that holds women in high regard is the Bhagwan Shree Rajneesh movement, also known as the Osho movement. In that group, women were also discouraged from having children as the movement's leader, Osho, stated that children were an obstacle in the way of women's spirituality (Guest, 2005). Children were given a high degree of self-determination. One of the consequences of this outlook is that attendance in boarding schools was voluntary (Puttick, 1999, p. 92).

Contemporary groups that reject parenthood altogether are also still around. One such example is The Church of Euthanasia on the internet, headed by Rev. Chris Corda. The only commandment of the group is: Thou shalt not procreate. The reason is that overpopulation of the planet hinders humankind from living compassionate and sustainable lives. The group further espouses birth control and abortion, and while not condoning suicide, they don't condemn it, seeing it as a successful way of saving the planet.

Celibacy and abstaining from sexual relations are the more common practice in the beginning of some movements' life cycle. Those that initially promote celibacy for all are confronted with the reality of having children anyway. Hence, they frequently reevaluate the doctrine of celibacy, transforming it to a practice for only a few selected members, such as Roman Catholic monks and nuns, or Hindu renunciates. A historical example can be found in the Shaker movement of the nineteenth century, which rejected sexual relations even within the frames of (Christian) marriage. In the case of the Shakers, children were either born by recently converted mothers, who had been pregnant upon admission, or came into the community via adoption. In some cases, newborns were left anonymously at the doorstep of the main house and were subsequently raised as members of the commune (Sobo & Bell, 2001). A recent example is found in the Hare Krishna movement, where the initial intention of founding a community of monks and nuns in celibacy in 1966 gradually developed into a predominantly householder community made up of nuclear families who took on the mission to provide for the small number of monks and nuns who served full time in the temples. However, due to the belief that abstinence from sexual relations is one of the most important principles (procreation is only for giving birth to Krishna-conscious children), there is still a hierarchical understanding of (male) celibacy, which is favored to the life of a householder (Rochford, 2007).

## Holy and Not-So-Holy Kids

Many parents, both members of new religions and those who are not, expect that their children will follow in the footsteps of their parents. This is not always something thought about, at least not until the terrain of the familiar is challenged by new experiences that are incongruent with former experiences. In the religious life world into which children in new religious movements are born, there are sometimes expectations for the children to be exceptionally spiritually developed. This seems to be connected to a belief that the new generation will be the one to bring about religious change, whatever it may be. For example, in the Family Federation for World Peace and Unification, known widely as the Unification Church, children were conceived in marriages typically arranged between a male and a female from different nations. The founder of the movement, Rev. Sun Myung Moon (1920–2012), was committed to uniting all Family Federation members (Mickler, 2022), and the chief way to accomplish this was to arrange large-scale weddings. The marriages have changed over time – going from the process where the leader would simply match the members, to most young adults now choosing whom to marry. Nevertheless, the strong emphasis on family and tradition means that many young members still turn to their parents to discuss marriage before making a decision. The strong emphasis on the nuclear family in Unificationism has its roots in a paradoxical aspect of the movement's main teachings. On the one hand, once the marriage is confirmed, the children born into that marriage are called "blessed children." These children are seen as the perfect manifestation of the cleansing of the bloodline that would ultimately lead to the coming unity of all the world's nations, under the leadership of Rev. Moon, who was believed to be the Messiah. On the other hand, some of the members came to the movement with children who had no way to become blessed with the pure bloodline. These children were typically seen as less spiritual, and the divide led some to feel less valuable to the movement (Åkerbäck, 2018).

The division between blessed and non-blessed children is found in several forms in other new religious movements. In COG/TFI, children were given the roles as the "Endtime" children and teens who would make up Jesus's army in the battle of Armageddon (Borowik, 2023). The Family was founded in 1968 by David Berg, a Christian preacher who started his movement by picking up lost teenagers and persuading them to reject drugs and accept Jesus instead. Initially, Berg preached celibacy for all, but as the movement grew, he received new prophecies that pointed toward a more liberal view on sexuality. Berg opposed the use of contraceptives, and as the movement grew, he increased his attacks against the shackles of nuclear family life. These teachings culminated in the doctrine of the Law of Love, a theological belief that justified sexual relations outside of the confines of marriage (Borowik, 2023, p. 24). Members could choose to have (heterosexual) sex with any member of the group who consented. Berg contended that the nuclear family was a threat to community and saw spousal monogamy as a form of societal greed. Because sex and sexuality were seen as holy, and sexual activity was increasing, so also was the population of children being born into the movement. Children were reared communally and generally, though not always, moved with their parents according to the dictates of leaders, and because of perceived and actual persecution. In the beginning, children were seen as pure and crucial to the battle of Armageddon. It was only when the second generation became teenagers that some started questioning the life that they had, up until then, considered their only world. The youth of the movement were divided into what Amanda van Eck Duymaer van Twist calls "goodies and baddies." The goodies were the ones who followed the rules and did not question the hierarchy or orders of the leaders, while the baddies were those who did, and who eventually left the movement (van Eck Duymaer van Twist, 2015).

The differentiation between goodies and baddies or blessed and non-blessed children is closely linked to the understanding of purity in new religious movements. However, the sacred/profane polarity should not be understood as monolithic but rather as complex (Paden, 1994). Within the system, several contrasting forms of the sacred can appear. In other words, the sacred may be relative within a religious community; moreover, religious worlds do not only vary between each other but can also vary within. Time as well as location are important factors in considering religious systems. What is deemed impure at a given point in history at a given place can be deemed pure or sacred at another point in history and in another place. The social boundaries of the religious world of the child in new religious movements is best understood by analyzing the presence of, and the interpretation and practical manifestation of, systems of purity. The key concept of purity is often an integral part of the life world of children (and adults) in new religions.

Building on the work of anthropologist Mary Douglas (1921–2007) in her classic *Purity and Danger* (2003), historian of religions William Paden suggests that religious systems deal with problems and negativity in three ways. A dualistic view of the world is significant for some new religious movements that divide the world into negative and positive realms. This dualism is prevalent in groups where strict social boundaries are employed, such as within the first decades of COG/TFI as well as the other new religions described in this Element. Paden asserts that the word "purity" is value-free, claiming that it merely denotes something that is "free from mixture or contact with that which weakens, impairs, or pollutes: containing no foreign or vitiating material" (Paden, 1994, p. 142). Every religious system has rules that separate the pure from the impure in the sense that certain actions lead to certain desirable goals, while others do not; some even lead to secular or supernatural punishment. Because of this separation of pure and impure and the very broad dictionary understanding of purity, it is usable in studies of new religious movements since it has a wide variety of applications to various levels of religious experience. The call for purity can encompass, for instance, dietary or cleanliness rules, but can also encompass inner personal forms of purity, such as self-renunciation or moral perfection according to the moral compass of the specific religious system (Paden, 1994).

The first way, avoidance of impurity, can be manifested in various prohibitions, stemming from organizational or hierarchical religious decrees; or it can be linked to personal efforts to avoid pollution, shame, or dishonor. The religious system can set up injunctions that are reinforced by threats of, for instance, supernatural punishment in this life or the next. Avoidance then stems from the fear of the consequences of mixing with the impure. A strikingly obvious example is the Jehovah's Witnesses avoidance of blood transfusion. George Chryssides observes that God's command to Noah that humans should eat meat but not if it contained blood (Genesis 1:30; 9:3–5) was first understood to refer to dietary uses only. It was after World War II that the interpretation of the passage to include blood banks circulated widely in the movement, since blood banks were rare before the 1940s (Chryssides, 2019). The question of blood transfusions in relation to children is often resolved by social authorities temporarily assuming the welfare of the child, to release the burden of the decision for the parents and to assure the child a blood transfusion if needed. However, various nations have their own rules regarding this. In Sweden, for instance, state authorities can assume temporary decision-making responsibility for the child if the parents refuse to cooperate with medical or other authorities; in other places, it remains the decision of the parents. Legal authority to consent or refuse treatment in the case of adolescents, sometimes leading to their death, has been granted, for example, in the State of New York. Over the years, the question of blood transfusions has led Jehovah's Witnesses to develop tools to make avoiding blood easier. In one case, specific blood parts are identified so that each type of blood or organ can be detailed on a donor card. Where members would normally carry a card stating that they refuse blood transfusion (including whole blood, red cells, white cells, platelets, and plasma) a No Blood app is now available for smartphones in case of emergency, for instance in case of accidents (https://apkpure.com/no-blood/com.csssounds.noblood).

A second category, according to Paden, deals with the response to impurity when it has already taken place. Cleansing an impure person or erasing guilt over a deed can be done in a variety of ways. Paden gives the following examples: punishment, banishment, shunning, use of scapegoats, exorcism, ritual combat, excommunication, required penance, imprisonment, pronounced forgiveness and pardon, and rehabilitation (Paden, 1994, pp. 154–5). The subject in need of purification may confess to his or her sins and try to make amends by way of fasting, prayer, or soul-searching. Sometimes certain natural elements conceived of as sacred – such as water, sun, rain, and so on – may play a role in the purification process. While the method of purification can be taken on by the individual, Paden stresses that there is always a system that specifies and promotes certain forms of purification for certain deeds. However, within the religious worlds of new religious movements, this is not always the case.

Knutby Filadelfia, a charismatic Christian new religious movement in Sweden, began in 1921 as a Christian Pentecostal congregation consisting of fewer than one hundred members. It only came to fit the description of new religious movements in the 1990s when, influenced by the Word of Life, the teachings turned increasingly charismatic. At the beginning of the twenty-first century, a prominent leader in the congregation identified the female charismatic leader of the congregation, Åsa Waldau, as the human incarnation of the Bride of Christ. These teachings were, however, only known to a small group within the congregation's inner core group.

The group became publicly known both nationally and internationally in January 2004 when a tragedy occurred. A member, Sara Svensson, shot and killed another member of the congregation, Alexandra Fossmo. Alexandra was the current wife of Pastor Helge Fossmo and the younger sister of Pastor Åsa Waldau. Another young member of the congregation was also shot by Svensson but survived.

Prior to the murder, Svensson had been engaged in a sexual relationship with Pastor Fossmo. Svensson had been banished from the congregation only three months prior to the attack. The police investigation soon showed that the murder had been ordered by text message from a source that Svensson thought was God but was identified to be Pastor Fossmo himself. The subsequent court case and sentencing of both Fossmo and Svensson showed some interesting details regarding Svensson's relation to Åsa Waldau and her position in the group at the time of the murder. Svensson had been shunned by Waldau some months prior to the murder, which meant that although she was physically still in the movement, no one but Helge Fossmo was allowed to talk to her.

In my thesis on the group's children and youth, I developed the term *spiritual shunning* to designate the spiritual component of social exclusion in the group

(Nilsson, 2019). This concept differs from the usual use of the concept of shunning within movements such as the Bruderhof (discussed in the following) or the Jehovah's Witnesses, where shunning (or disfellowshipping in their terms) means physically leaving the community. Svensson was shunned because she was deemed spiritually impure, and the fear that she might contaminate the charismatic leader was given as a cause. Although Svensson was ultimately ordered to leave the congregation, most cases of shunning took place within the active congregation. However, when I interviewed children and youth in the movement between 2014 and 2018 (the congregation officially broke up in 2018), it became clear that social exclusion was less predictable than Paden suggested in his theory.

The reasons for spiritual shunning in this case were closely connected to the charismatic leaders. By the time of my research in 2011, a pastor named Urban Fält had filled Fossmo's place and acted as Waldau's primary confidante. In the movement's lingo, members had to "stand right" with both Waldau and Fält. The definition of standing right, however, was far from clear. In several cases, Waldau would expect a particular member to behave in a certain way on a certain day but would not disclose to the member what the proper action for the day was. Additionally, members primarily of the inner circle close to the leadership could find themselves in social exclusion without knowing either what had caused it or how to redeem themselves. Similarly, sometimes the shunning would suddenly stop without any reason given. Consequently, many of the members of the leadership cadre were on a constant watch out for inner and/or outer impure behavior, trying to prevent the shunning.

Approximately fifteen teenagers and young adults (aged twelve to twenty-five) came to make up a youth group, modeled largely on the inner circle of the adults. The members of the youth group were held in quite high esteem and had access to the charismatic leaders in a way that most congregational members did not, regardless of age. They developed a similar structure, including spiritual shunning as a disciplining method when any of the youth had (or were believed to have) behaved in profane ways. Interestingly, members of the youth group could unknowingly impact the spiritual shunning of adult members. A stray accusation or critique from one of the youths could have serious consequences. One such example was when an adult member of the inner core group was ordered away from his family to live for months in a shack because one of the teens had mentioned suspicions in passing that he was unfaithful to his spouse. The teen was unaware of the consequences until the congregation broke up. In another case, a mother was shunned for several years while her children, who belonged to the youth group, were sneered at by their peers for having such an impure parent. This, of course, created a power imbalance between the mother and her children, in which the children felt embarrassed by the transgressions of the parent, while the parent had not even been given an explanation for the shunning in the first place (Nilsson, 2019).

Another example of a movement dealing with systems of purity is the Bruderhof, an Anabaptist-inspired group of pietist communities living in their own villages. Founded in the 1920s in Germany, the community spread to parts of the English-speaking world fleeing World War II. A schism occurred in the 1960s (referred to as The Great Crisis within the movement), when the community was divided into those who favored isolation and becoming self-sustaining, and those who sought working relations with the surrounding society. Several adult members were expelled from the group favoring more engagement with the world because they criticized the turn of the group from pietistic to merely communal. Although the parents were (temporarily) banished, the children were invited to stay on the basis of being so-called *sabra youth*. Children in the Bruderhof are referred to as *sabras* or *sabra youth*, denoting their purity as children having been born into a peaceful community. The children are seen as so special that they need to be kept from the potentially polluting influences from mainstream society. The remaining adults effectively became a rather closed community. The ousted members were eventually let back in, but the schism led many to leave the communities (van Eck Duymaer van Twist, 2015).

Paden's third and final category describes the strategy that some groups employ in response to impurity: transcending the pure/impure dichotomy. Paden suggests that within some religious systems, efforts are made to transcend the division of good and evil, which is significant for a large portion of the religious world. This can be done by accepting an impure part, or by trying to invest it with purity. An example given is of the left-hand path of Tantric yoga, which emphasizes participation in acts that are, within Tantrism, otherwise seen as unclean, such as eating meat or drinking alcohol (Paden, 1994, p. 157). Another example in which impurity becomes irrelevant is the bhakti yoga tradition practiced through hugs within the Mata Amritanandamayi Math, a movement surrounding female guru Sri Mata Amritanandamamayi Devi (known as Amma). Devotees of Amma presumably keep their original faith but add elements from Amma's teachings. Tøllefsen and Giudice describe the personal embraces that form the core of the practice, in which the guru transcends the opposition of pure and impure (Tøllefsen & Giudice, 2017).

There can also be a view of purity that is enhanced in relation to the profane world. Hence, within some religious systems, a person can live within the profane world while staying pure on the inside. This is illustrated by the words of Titus in the New Testament (Titus 1:15, KJV), "Unto the pure all things are pure." Verse 9.30 in the Bhagavad Gita says something similar: "Even if one commits the most abominable action, if he is engaged in devotional service, he is to be considered saintly because he is properly situated in his determination" (Bhaktivedanta, 2006). The idea that certain godly persons (mostly men) can transcend the impurity of this world while remaining in it has sometimes been used as an argument to justify unlawful treatment of children in some new religious movements. We will revisit this subject in Section 6.

The pure/impure division is sometimes detectable in societal and/or communal views about children. Child studies scholar Chris Jenks uses two mythological – that is, metaphorical – images, *Apollonian* and *Dionysian*, to conceptualize contrasting views of children and childhood (Jenks, 2005). The image of childhood through the Dionysian lens sees the child as intrinsically chaotic and potentially evil. Dionysus is the uncontrolled, emotional son of Zeus who engages in ecstatic dancing while intoxicated by excessive wine drinking. When applied to childhood, the assumption is that such a child must be constrained and controlled; otherwise, it will inevitably end up in bad company and develop demonic traits that could hurt the whole community. The child is susceptible to all kinds of immoral behavior, and this has, through the history of childhood, seemed to require or promote such practices as swaddling and corporal punishment. This view of children can be linked to a Christian perspective where the concept of original sin gave rise to a system of raising children in the spirit of absolute obedience. Jenks points to the fact that this image of childhood is present in the most influential theory of childhood used in the Western world today, namely Freud's notion of the id (Jenks, 2005, p. 64). The Dionysian child is visible in social structures that favor uniformity over individualism. Transgressions are punished and Jenks writes that: "Real children in such a society sacrifice their childhood to the cause of the collective adult good. As a result of such control the growing individual learns a respect for society through the experience of shame" (Jenks, 2005, p. 70).

The Apollonian image of childhood, on the other hand, is guided by reason and dreams. The Apollonian child stands for a romanticized innocence, an intrinsic purity paired with altruistic goodness; the child becomes the vessel for parental idolization and almost worship. Jenks sees this view of childhood as dominant in our contemporary Western world, where childhood is a desirable dream state surrounded by nostalgic radiance. In this view, children are distinctively different from adults and are treated as individuals in their own right. Jenks further relates the historical transition from a Dionysian to an Apollonian view of childhood through mythical images to Foucault's notions of changes in discipline – from punishment to treatment. According to Jenks, this in turn coincides with other changes in society at the same time (the mid-eighteenth century) in such social institutions as schools and hospitals (Jenks, 2005, p. 66). There is, in Foucault's analysis, a spatial and temporal strategy of control that situates, in this case, the child's body in a specific location and divides its day into certain activities. Childhood occurs in a series of stages culminating in adulthood and emerging out of "patterns of constraint" dictated by the community (Jenks, 2005, p. 68). The contemporary child is Apollonian, growing up in a social structure signified by panopticism, which insinuates subtle forms of control and an increasing individualization. Though this shift from Dionysian to Apollonian might seem simplistic, it does mirror changes in the overall societal structure. While Jenks cautions us not to understand the two concepts as stemming from cultural regimes such as religions only, as they are no longer relevant, he does point to the fact that they are at times enforced by religions and political ideologies.

## 3 Socialization and Social Relations: Family Life in the Religious Life World of the Child

Social relations are a set of cultural constructions transmitted to the individual by family, friends, peers, and teachers where the significance of everyday life language is an integral part of cultural socialization. Typologies denoting specific aspects of cultural life are often group specific (Schutz, 1967, p. 39). The concept of life world is used here to illustrate everyday life for children in some new religious movements, as the life world is the basis of the individual's reality. The world in what sociologist Alfred Schutz terms *the natural attitude* is an intersubjective world, where practical interests rule. Theoretical knowledge has no place in the natural attitude. The natural attitude within the life world facilitates communication between individuals who inhabit the same life world. Communication is closely connected to symbols and tokens, which have a given way of interpretation (Schutz, 1967, p. 79). In new religions, a common interpretation of concepts may differ from their mainstream interpretation. When leaders of COG/TFI decided to do what they called a "reboot" of the organization in 2010, they sent out a list of words and phrases used *within* the group. The list explained the common usage and meaning of the words in society *outside* the group. Because members, especially those belonging to the inner circle of the movement, had been homeschooled, socially isolated, and not encouraged to attend higher education, many of the second generation had to relearn the concepts' original or actual meaning, now that the group planned enhanced interaction with society (Nilsson, 2011). One term that was redefined was "dating," which within the group mostly included sex; this was not the case outside the group. Other words and concepts had originated in the interpretation of theology, for instance, "babe" which meant a new convert (1 Peter 2:2 and 1 Cor 3:1); or Romans, referring to the Roman persecution of Christians and meaning police or authority figures. In groups coming from other nations and cultures, specific words from the language of that culture are integrated into the language of the group. The use of Hindi expressions in the Hare Krishnas is one such example. *Karmis* denotes people who act to satisfy their senses rather than out of devotion, *mleccha* similarly points to persons outside the social and spiritual divisions of Vedic culture, whose practices are considered sinful. *Prasada* is sanctified food. I have found that accumulating some of these in-group phrases of a movement is helpful when researching young children, since the risk of misinterpretation should not be underestimated.

Given that communication and interaction within the life world is facilitated by common horizons of knowledge, the boundaries of the life world can keep out knowledge of society beyond the inhabited life world of the group. In this sense, the limits of a person's life world complicate knowledge beyond the theoretical level. According to Schutz and Luckmann, the individual is free to act within this realm only to a certain extent, as he or she is always subjected to the actions of, and the interaction with, fellow human beings (Schutz & Luckmann, 1973, p. 3). However, within the life world, the natural attitude is to assume that actions and events taking place in the outer world are interpreted by others in the same way we ourselves interpret them. This is the common ground for communication in the natural attitude. Within the life world of children, then, young children take for granted that others live by the same rules as they do. This is evident in life stories from adults who grew up in new religious movements but attended regular school. This encounter with the outside world is overwhelming to many children, but those in new religions add that, depending on the degree of social isolation of the group, the decoding of outside language, especially regarding children's culture, could be difficult. Children take their everyday lives for granted, as they tend to inhabit one or fewer life worlds. The province of the familiar for children within new religions may differ from their peers, something several children I have interviewed have encountered when attending regular schools. Common cultural references take time to learn, and sometimes interviewees note how they developed two quite differing personas – one for the religious socialization at home and in the group and one for peer-socialization at school. To some, the shifting between life worlds with radically different expectations would be exhausting, while for others it is a way of coping that they felt worked out quite well.

The life world is dynamic and ever-changing. Thus, we are in constant interaction with the world, which gives a reciprocal two-way influence: Our actions affect the life world, and at the same time, the life world affects our actions. Knowledge within the life world is based on previous experience, and action is navigated by a reference schema that categorizes objects and events according to previous knowledge (Schutz & Luckmann, 1973, p. 7). Despite the dynamics of the life world, it appears as constant to the individual. This is why certain action is calculated to have a certain outcome based on previous outcomes, an assumption clearly made out of the understanding of the life world as constant, as a "province of the familiar" (Schutz & Luckmann, 1973, p. 9). However, as we have seen, this is not always the case.

## Everybody's Children, Nobody's Parents? Communal Socialization

The socialization of children in new religions takes on a variety of forms. Some groups advocate communal fostering of all children, some leave the socialization to the parents (typically within nuclear family units), and still others reject having children altogether. Additionally, as frequent change is common within these groups, norms may vary over time. With roots in utopian communes, however, child-rearing in new religious movements has tended to be experimental. Some groups start out with the idea of celibacy for all its members or accept reproduction only with the intent to bear children, while others maintain that childbearing is a hindrance to spiritual development. The latter idea can be found in some of the utopian communes of the nineteenth century, such as the Oneida Perfectionists discussed earlier.

The separation of children and parents has been, and is still to some extent, present in several new religions. The reasons vary, but every so often parents needed in the work for the movement are deemed unfit or as a threat to the child's spiritual growth and purity, or both (Lalich & McLaren, 2018). As noted, children are frequently perceived as being spiritually purer than their parents, especially if they are born into the group. Communal raising of children was more accepted by the mainstream during the 1960s and 1970s, however, as it followed a general development in society. Subsequently, the process of individualization of society in the 1980s led to a more child-centered paradigm focused on the nuclear family as the economic unit; previous communal arrangements were criticized. One might say that new religious movements followed that development to some extent, but with a general delay of ten to twenty years.

The active presence of parents or primary caretakers tends to result in successful socialization, while their absence tends to leave the child with a feeling of rootlessness. Regarding the separation of children and parents in new religious movements, Siskind found that when parents were required to work for the organization, it sometimes resulted in a feeling of loss for the child (Siskind, 2001). I discovered in my study of the Knutby Filadelfia movement that children were sometimes placed with other families. The reasons given were that the parents were needed in the community work, or they had prominent positions taking care of the charismatic leader. In a few cases, parents (especially mothers) were deemed a bad influence on the child, and therefore raised by another female member. Reflecting in hindsight, parents said they had limited contact with their children, being unable to see them grow up; at the same time, the arrangement had felt safe since it meant that the child was secure and well taken care of by someone whose primary purpose was not to serve the leader (Nilsson, 2019). To entrust a child into the care of boarding schools of religions has several times proven harmful, both within the realm of new religions and outside of it, as we can see in the history of abuse in the Roman Catholic boarding schools for indigenous children. Yet, communal socialization can be very beneficial for the child if (s)he develops close bonds to other adults within the movement. It may present a refuge of safety for a child whose parents are in some sense not stable or adequately performing their parental roles.

Socialization encompasses the transmission of rules, values, norms, and regulations. Younger children have a higher need for predictability through recurring routines and foreseeable outcomes of certain behavior. There may be rules regarding how to dress, what to eat, and how to speak that provide behavioral cues (Grusec & Davidov, 2007, p. 299). Most of the children I have met, observed, and interviewed state that they had not questioned their parents' request that they attend regular religious gatherings until they became teenagers, and some never did at all (Nilsson, 2019). It was just understood as a part of life, as recurring and regulated as breakfast, sleeping time, or taking a shower. Parents often try to connect the gatherings with something that the children will feel is fun. It may be the sheer fact of meeting friends within the group, but it may also be special activities directed at the children while simultaneously transmitting the values of the faith of the group. For the children of Knutby Filadelfia, regular summer camps were arranged by the youth of the congregation for the younger children. Involving them in role-play to illustrate proper behavior and challenges directed at increasing their theological knowledge constituted secondary socialization. The importance of peer socialization is sometimes lost in the debates over religious socialization. Studies show that as children grow, the secondary socialization provided by school, teachers, and peers exceeds that of their parents (Arnett, 2007). Children brought up in the Unification Church, for example, described the year they spent in South Korea, which is common among youth within the group, as especially valuable to their religious socialization.

Some young adults who grow up in new religious movements express gratitude for having been socialized into a sense of belonging and into a meaningful life in regard to their faith. They feel that their identities were based on clear and solid role models, distinct rules governing behavior, and that they feel chosen for important work through the beliefs of the group. Others recount their identity building period within the group as restraining, inflexible, and surrounded by rules that, when broken, left them feeling worthless and doubting themselves. Identity is built on role models and imitation processes are an important part of socialization. When the role models seem to be unattainable, the expectations can be experienced as too heavy. Often, role models are not solely parents or religious leaders but older peers within the movement and other adult members. Some of the children and youth that I have met throughout my studies have explained that while they may not be forbidden (in the strict sense of the word) to socialize with peers from school, they choose to spend their time with friends and family within the movement, because they identify with them more. They don't feel the need to explain themselves and the way they live, dress, eat, and talk. I have, however, met youth that were disappointed because they were discouraged from participating in after-school activities as they had wished because their parents, and sometimes leaders, considered the activities to be too worldly or the mixing with outsiders to have negative impacts in the youths' identities (Nilsson, 2019).

## 4 Education

Rodney Stark (1996) has pointed out that the success rate of a new religion surviving depends on the socialization and retention of the second and further generations of children. One way to effectively socialize children into the cultural and social construct of the movement's beliefs and values is through education. The nature of education for children in new religious movements is varied and has changed within the movements over time. Separate religious education schools are set up in order to maintain the boundaries between what is understood as pure and impure, to shield the child from what is perceived of as the harm of the profane world.

The Plymouth Brethren Christian Church, popularly known as The Exclusive Brethren, is a Christian evangelical group founded in 1848 when they split from the major Brethren congregations, the latter of which are now known as the Open Brethren. The faith and lifestyle of the Exclusive Brethren differs from the Open Brethren in that they emphasize a doctrine of separation from the world, which is most notably identified as separation from nonmembers. This is manifested in members not sharing food with nonmembers, as each meal is considered to some degree to present The Lord's Supper. They do not take part in any activities of different organizations and associations such as sports clubs, worker's unions, or activities that are organized by any other entity than the church.

The group has a global organization called OneSchool Global, which administers the movement's schools in different countries. The pupils are generally members of the group, although some schools do accept other pupils as well. As of 2007, the Exclusive Brethren have a school in Sweden that has been the focus of many discussions about what is labeled a "cult school." The news media and individual politicians repeatedly have tried to get school inspectors to revoke permission for the school to operate but have not yet succeeded. As the school offers education only from grade 3 through 9, children of members of the Exclusive Brethren in Sweden have to attend their first three years in public schools. When interviewed about their experiences of attending public school, the children recounted a variety of experiences. They were not encouraged to associate with peers outside school hours, and would not participate in excursions involving sleepovers, but several maintained that they felt they had managed just fine anyway. A few mentioned being bullied for having "too formal clothes" and they stated that while it was not pleasant, they always had friends from the congregation to associate with after school and felt that this helped them to cope. All the children and youth interviewed stated that they felt that they were relieved to transfer to the movement's school, as they could associate with children of their own, familiar, culture. Children are not encouraged to obtain higher education, but there are of course a few exceptions. Because the Exclusive Brethren tend to run successful industrial companies making useful products – such as building materials, hygiene items, packing goods – there will be plenty of job opportunities. Women are homemakers but can help out in the businesses. Movement-run schools seem to serve as safe places for the group's children.

The practice of not eating with nonmembers, and the fact that girls and women always wear long hair and skirts, are significant differences that are directly visible to other children. At Nyby school, the teachers eat lunch in a room adjacent to the room where the pupils eat (there is no door in between) so that they can keep an eye on them while still observing the desire of the parents that their children do not eat – "break bread" – with nonmembers. The Swedish School Inspectorate has scrutinized the school several times, since reports from media and outsiders critical of what they call a "cult school" keep reappearing. The criticism is centered on teachers not being adequately educated, the separation of sexes, and the fostering of patriarchal gender roles. In the summer of 2022, the Swedish School Inspectorate claimed that the school had been separating boys and girls during physical education, something that is not legal in Sweden. The school immediately corrected this problem, and when I visited in November that same year, I was invited to see a mixed physical education class. Another complaint that the school received in 2022 was that there had not been any sex education classes for two years. The school claimed that this was due to a misunderstanding between teachers when one teacher was replaced with another. While interviewing adult representatives from the school board, the question of sex education was problematized. The Swedish National Curriculum states that teachers are to be prepared to speak to pupils on the subject whenever they bring it up, not only during a specific course. The parents on the school board claimed that while they would not discourage teachers from following this rule, they stated that they felt uneasy at the thought, explaining that the members of the Brethren consider transmission of this form of knowledge to be the responsibility of parents, prior to marriage, not in elementary school (Frisk & Nilsson, 2021).

The Jehovah's Witnesses, on the other hand, trust that the child can keep pure within a secular school system. Generally, the organization encourages its children to witness to peers but discourages them from forming social relations outside of school hours with nonmembers. The children do not participate in religiously motivated activities, such as celebrations around Christmas or birthdays (Chryssides, 2016). Some adult children report that this nonparticipation could feel embarrassing and that it was hard growing up as a Jehovah's Witness in the public school system; others, however, have felt superior through identifying with an elite group and seen it as their privilege to be Witnesses. Like the Exclusive Brethren, many children within the Jehovah's Witnesses relate that they have had a wide range of brothers and sisters in the congregation to turn to (Liedgren, 2007, p. 396). Of course, every rule has its exceptions, and children and parents can be very creative in obtaining things that they are not given. Interviews show that when parents would oppose the leadership's opinion – for example, by enrolling their child in an after-school activity outside of the congregation – they would pay by having their status in the group lowered (Frisk, 2018a). Moreover, children might feel ashamed or even afraid when they engaged in activities in school that their parents did not know about.

Pratezina describes her experience of growing up in the religious commune the Worldwide Church of God in relation to not being permitted to participate in certain celebrations that are common to many children, such as Halloween. She describes the paradox of experiencing both excitement and fear when her mother would have the children hide on the floor and not open the door when anyone knocked (Pratezina, 2021, p. 8). She further recounts how in the initial phases of her gradual defection from the group, the family of her nonmember friends would attempt to "save her." This was very upsetting to her, as she had been taught (and still believed) that the religion of her friends was dangerous (Pratezina, 2021, p. 9).

## Boarding Schools

Boarding schools of all sorts may have problems maintaining safety and security for all children while their parents are not present, yet there are examples of religiously based boarding schools that function very well. When it comes to the schools run by new religious movements, however, one of their key features is that they tend to experiment with norms and to create their own traditions. In some cases, these experiments have backfired in a way that has had consequences for children of several generations. Consider, for instance, the *gurukulas* (boarding schools) of the Hare Krishna movement which were founded on the idea that the emotional attachment to parents could jeopardize the child's spiritual development (Rochford, 2007; Burt, 2023). Divided most commonly into boys and girls schools, the first gurukula was started in Dallas, Texas in 1971 (Wolf, 2004, p. 322) The gurukula was a school where children aged five and older lived with their teacher/s and other children. There were several reasons for the foundation of gurukulas in the West. On the one hand, it is a common system in India, and on the other hand, there was an idea from the founder, A. C. Bhaktivedanta Swami Prabhupada (1896–1977), that parents should leave their children so that children could be trained in Krishna consciousness without being disturbed by their parents' attachment, which they were told were "ropes of attachment" (van Eck Duymaer van Twist, 2015, pp. 54–5). Another aspect that ISKCON – the International Society of Krishna Consciousness, the institutional branch of the Hare Krishnas – shares with many missionary religious movements is the understanding that parents need to be relieved from their parental responsibility so that they can travel on missions, working for the movement. There was also an understanding that the children were "Krishna's children," thus children of the movement rather than children of the biological parents.

Former *gurukulis* – adults who attended gurukula as children and/or teenagers – argue that when the children became everyone's children, they at the same time became nobody's children in terms of individual responsibility. Although many parents believed that the gurukula system was the best option for their children, some felt pressured to sign their children into the system against their will; some were even threatened with expulsion from the temple by religious officials if they refused. Many parents were encouraged to send their sons to movement schools in India, usually at a young age. A Swedish case where a young boy was sent to a school in India by himself is documented in Daniel Lutz's autobiographical book *My Karma, My Fault* (2010). Rochford and Heinlein write that because the children were seen as an obstacle to the parents' ability to make money for the movement, a well-known expression regarding the children as obstacles was "dump the load and hit the road." The vast majority who were assigned to teach in the movement's schools were members who were not considered "good enough" to preach and/or make money and were often completely uneducated. The schools of the movement therefore became institutions characterized by isolation and marginalization (Rochford with Heinlein, 1998, p. 53).

For his book *Hare Krishna Transformed* (2007), Rochford interviewed second-generation members about sexual exploitation, corporal punishment, poor health-care, and mental abuse in the movement's gurukulas. It seems to have been worse in the movement's schools in India, where the culture of abuse was taken over by the children, and older boys exploited younger ones. Rochford's research suggests that as many as 20 percent of all children who participated in the gurukula system may have been abused, with up to almost 75 percent of all boys who attended the gurukula in Vrindavan, India (Rochford, 2007, p. 75). In the 1980s, a two-year-old boy died after being subjected to physical punishment in the movement's gurukula in New Vrindavan, West Virginia, where two small boys also died after being left in a freezer. It was discovered that two gurus, Kirtanananda and Bhavananda, had sexually abused children in New Vrindavan (Van Eck Duymaer Van Twist, 2015, p. 56). In 1984, child abuse was also discovered in the movement's gurukula in Los Angeles. By 1986, most ashram-based schools were closed except for schools in India (Rochford with Heinlein, 1998, pp. 46–7). Despite indications that physical and sexual abuse of children occurred, the shortcomings of the gurukula system did not become public knowledge until former students began to speak openly in the 1990s about their experiences with gurukulas.

In June 2000, forty-four former students sued ISKCON for $400 million for physical, emotional, and sexual abuse within the gurukula in the high-profile Windle Turley case. By May 2003, the number of complainants had risen to ninety-one. The lawsuit resulted in a financial settlement because the organization applied for bankruptcy, which nullified the possibility of legal action. The damages, totaling $9.5 million, were distributed among 535 former gurukula students to compensate for their suffering. ISKCON also promised to contact all former students who went to gurukulas and published an apology to them (Burt, 2023, pp. 54–5). The former students organized themselves during the 1990s through recurring meetings where several complained that without a trial, they felt "bought off" rather than compensated. Their complaints were met with some criticism from the organization. In his "Letter of Me," Anuttama Dasa, who was then the organization's chief spokesperson and later served as education manager, acknowledged that abuse had taken place, but that he opposed the continued criticism. He said that ISKCON had taken measures to prevent future abuse and that the abuse had been committed by individuals who did not follow the religious principles of Swami Prabhupada and the movement (van Eck Duymaer van Twist, 2015, p. 57).

Pointing out individual perpetrators rather than seeing the structural problems did not appease the previous students. Former gurukuli Raghunatha Anudasa responded to Anuttama Dasa's statement that the measures taken were only superficial and did not in any way acknowledge the seriousness of what they had been subjected to. He further claimed that a large part of the financial resources allocated to the work with child safety went to administrative costs and that his generation was never allowed to comment on the person responsible, the Minister for Youth within ISKCON, whom he considered "useless" (van Eck Duymaer van Twist, 2015, p. 58). Many former gurukulis, like Raghunatha Anudasa, felt abandoned by the leadership's way of sweeping the problems under the rug, as they saw it, which led to many second-generation members leaving the organization. Although the Windle Turley case led to the establishment of a child protection institution, the movement still had its battles with accusations of abuse in the gurukulas located in India and Russia. In response to this, the Child Protection Office (CPO) was established in 1990. (See Section 6 for ISKCON's response to charges of abuse.)

Some movements develop a pedagogy that may initially receive criticism but which, after some time, spreads to schools not closely affiliated with the movement. The Waldorf schools build upon on the pedagogy of Rudolf Steiner (1861–1925), a Theosophist who, discontented with the development of Theosophy, founded his own movement in 1912: the Anthroposophical Society. The first Waldorf school was established in 1919 and since then, they have spread all over the globe, with approximately 900 schools worldwide in 2023. The Waldorf pedagogy developed by Steiner was based on his anthroposophical ideas, which include a theory of children's development as occurring in three phases. In each seven-year phase, the child is receptive to certain types of knowledge and instruction, according to their age. Between the ages of birth to seven, the child's development centers around curiosity; between seven and fourteen, the willingness to learn; and between fourteen and twenty-one the exploration and understanding of moral divisions between right and wrong. In the second phase, seven to fourteen, it is imperative that the teacher act as a role model and authority for the child. Because of this, the Steiner schools tend to have a single teacher follow the child throughout the second phase, and only take in other teachers when needed for a specific subject (Frisk, 2018b; Swartz, 2022).

Waldorf schools differ somewhat in terms of how closely Steiner's teachings are followed, but tend to emphasize ecology and farming, as they are closely linked to the ideas of Steiner regarding agriculture. Most schools have a Steiner seminar where teachers read and discuss Steiner's texts on pedagogy, which are full of references to spiritual knowledge and development. Steiner initially insisted that children be taught religion class according to the faith of their parents; however, the educational curricula in some countries require that all children learn about all religions. Steiner's approach to Christianity differs from the mainstream, but the stories in the Bible do play an important role in his educational program. Waldorf schools typically use what is called "morning speech," which is a sort of poem written by Steiner, illustrating the virtues considered important:

> Admire the beautiful
> and love the true
> Decide on the good
> and revere the noble
> That leads us human beings toward a true goal in life
> To right in our action,
> to peace in our feeling,
> to light in our thought
> And teaches us to perceive that everywhere exists
> the prevailing wisdom of God
> In the space of everything,
> in the foundation of the soul. (Translation by Frisk, 2018b)

Additionally, there are a few festivals throughout the year that are usually held in the Waldorf schools. There is Michaelmas in the autumn, which celebrates the archangel, Michael. If the school has its own garden or farmland, harvest is celebrated. Handicraft is another important part of the education since Steiner emphasizes the cognitive connection between the movements of the hands and learning. Waldorf schools are open to all children, and sometimes attract pupils from new religions, such as the Hare Krishnas and other new spiritual practitioners because it serves mainly vegetarian, environmentally sound food, and propagates and teaches thoughtful responses to climate change and values education outdoors (Nilsson, 2010). The schools have been met with criticism, as their curricula's focus on handicraft leave less time for subjects that are favored by mainstream public schools, such as mathematics and reading. It has similarly been criticized for its religious content and its emphasis on spirituality (Stehlik, 2019).

Another pedagogy that has received similar criticism is the "study tech" of Applied Scholastics, originally developed by the founder of the Church of Scientology, L. Ron Hubbard (1911–1986). Hubbard viewed children as adults in small bodies, with a firm belief in the child's right to self-determination based on the philosophy of Dianetics, which teaches that humans are thetans (souls) imprisoned in human bodies (Westbrook, 2022). Learning is a way of understanding one's true identity. The foundation of Hubbard's theory is that learning is a process that should be gradual. He pointed to three barriers to learning. The first is the absence of mass. This means that if there is no physical representation of what is being learned, it will be harder to understand. The second barrier is a steep study gradient, which means that one or more steps in the learning process were skipped. Lastly, misunderstanding words may disrupt the educational process. Some words have different meaning according to context, or the student simply does not know the meaning of the word and should therefore stop to look up the proper definition in a dictionary. A misunderstood word is most often the problem when a student pauses in his or her reading. While the Church of Scientology asserts that Applied Scholastics is a nonreligious method, it has been criticized for being a cover for indoctrination into Scientology (or rather Dianetics) of children without their parents' consent.

Children of Scientologists attend nonconfessional private or independent schools that use the Applied Scholastics program (for instance, Delphi Schools) or ordinary schools. For children whose parents are members of the SeaOrg inner group, there were so-called Cadet Schools, boarding schools operating between the early 1970s and 2000. The SeaOrg generally comprises prominent members of the Church of Scientology; but when they have children, they have to put their position at the SeaOrg on hold. Like the SeaOrg, members of the CadetOrg lived communally. If a child left the CadetOrg, the parent became disqualified as a member of the SeaOrg (van Eck Duymaer van Twist, 2015, 157).

As illustrated by these examples, new religious movements have a variety of ways of educating their children. Some believe that separating the movement's children from what they perceive to be an impure surrounding society is the best way to guard against defection and minimize the risks of influence from mainstream society. Others urge their young ones to participate in public schooling as it prepares them for interaction with the outside world and sees engagement in public education as a chance for the children to witness other children. Still others may have a preferred way of educating the young but are unable due to national prohibitions regarding homeschooling and/or confessional schools. In many of the groups, the view on ways of educating the movement's children is subject to continuous change.

## 5 Healthcare

As with education, issues regarding health have sometimes sparked controversies over new religions. These may concern reluctance to seek out professional medical assistance in cases where children would have needed such, or the practice of unconventional ways of treating illness, for instance by praying or other healing practices. While it is important to recognize that most groups do make use of conventional health institutions, at least to some extent, it is typically the cases where refusal to do so has had profound or even deadly consequences that are often highlighted in accounts of new religions. The phenomena of Indigo and Crystal Children, along with Scientology's approach to medicine (particularly mental health), are two examples of groups that have evoked controversy.

## The Indigo and Crystal Children

The categories of Indigo Children and Crystal Children come from the New Age environment and identify children with various extraordinary abilities. It is a bit difficult to get a general grasp on this because there is no clearly defined movement, but rather a number of ideas that circulate in certain new religious milieus. The term Indigo Children seems to have first been used by Nancy Ann Tappe (1931–2012), a writer of parapsychology in the 1970s, who developed her thoughts based on colorology, the study of the influence of colors. One of her students, Barbara Bowers, published the widely sold *What Color Is Your Aura?: Personality Spectrums for Understanding and Growth* (1989). Both Tappe and Bowers claimed that many children who were born in the 1970s and 1980s were born with an indigo blue aura, which, according to that teaching, had certain characteristics. The concept of Indigo Children was further popularized in the 1990s through several books where these children were sometimes described as the new evolutionary step in human development, sometimes as having certain abilities such as telepathy, but often as being extra empathic and extremely creative. Books regarding the subject include *The Indigo Children: The New Kids Have Arrived* (1998), written by self-help gurus Lee Carroll and Jan Tober, and Steve Rother's concept of Crystal Children in *Re-Member: A Handbook for Human Evolution* (2000). Doreen Virtue took this further in *The Crystal Children: A Guide to the Newest Generation of Psychic and Sensitive Children* (2003) as did Agneta Strandberg in *Children and Spirituality: Guidance Manual for Parents of Children Who See, Hear and Feel Energies from Other Dimensions* (2017). These publications, along with others, helped popularize and keep the terms topical in new spiritual circles.

Children born between the 1970s and 1990s are sometimes called Indigo Children, while Crystal Children refers to the later generations, born in the 1990s and 2000s. Some believe that the first wave of Indigo Children was actually born in the 1950s, but their attempts at bettering the world were not successful. The common notion for all generations is their intention, and later, capacity, to change the world with love. The generations of the Indigo Children are sometimes called "system breakers" as their endeavor is to change the world (the systems) with love by fighting against any actions and attitudes that are not based in love. These children are described as strong willed and honest (Singler, 2015). The Crystal Children's characteristics are that they seek balance between irrationality and intuition and that they have a more healing mission than the Indigo Children. The Crystal Children move between unusually high levels of consciousness and are extremely sensitive to so-called low vibrations. A Crystal Child is part of a generation that promises to intervene in the world through love, peace, and harmony.

Concepts such as high sensitivity people and neuro divergency – attention deficit hyperactivity disorder (ADHD) and attention deficit disorder – have been discussed in the twenty-first century regarding the belief in Indigo and Crystal Children. This is interesting because in many cases it appears to function as an explanatory model for why some children seem unable to conform to the norms and expectations of society. Sarah W. Whedon suggests in her 2009 article "The Wisdom of Indigo Children: An Emphatic Restatement of the Value of American Children" that the social construction of Indigo Children is a response to what she terms a crisis of American childhood in the form of increased youth violence and diagnoses of ADHD. Whedon argues that parents chose to label their children as Indigo Children to provide a new explanation for their children's improper behavior, which is triggered by the ADHD (Whedon, 2009). Critics further believe that the idea of specially gifted children might present a way for parents to avoid medications aimed at the symptoms, as these are understood to potentially harm the child's unique abilities. Autism researcher Mitzi Waltz, who has linked the concept of Crystal Children to the autism spectrum, argues that advocates recategorize autistic symptoms as telepathic powers, and attempt to reconceptualize "the autistic traits associated with them as part of a positive identity" (Waltz, 2009, p. 124). She believes that there may be dangers to these beliefs, leading parents to deny the existence of impairments, avoid proven treatments, and spend considerable money on unhelpful interventions.

## Mental Health

One of the most controversial approaches to healthcare comes from the Church of Scientology, which differs from mainstream Western medicine, not least in the realm of mental illnesses. The foundation of Scientology is the development of Dianetics, a therapeutic model for psychological healing. The religion is based on the belief that each individual is a thetan – the true self, which is considered to be immortal (Westbrook, 2022). However, humans are constantly subjected to traumatic events that leave what Scientologists call engrams, negative ripples, or patterns in the mind, which prevent the thetan from fulfilling its full potential. The traumatic events can be anything from simply being born, to injuries, large and small. To erase the tracks of the engrams, Dianetics uses the process called auditing to find and heal the engrams. Auditing is performed with the help of an e-meter, a device like a lie detector but unique to the Church of Scientology. The e-meter finds the engrams and by a method resembling exposure to trauma – as utilized within other therapeutic treatments – the Scientologist retells and relives the trauma until it stops causing traumatic feelings. In the case of Dianetics, the level of feeling is graphically indicated by the e-meter.

L. Ron Hubbard stated that at least 70 percent of all diseases are psychosomatic and can thus be cured by auditing. This goes for variations of mental illnesses as well, which has prompted the Church of Scientology to campaign quite vigorously against the use of psychotropic medications. There is no comprehensive comparative study on the usage of psychoactive drugs related to ADHD and autism in children in comparison with children growing up without parents adhering to the beliefs of Scientology. Apart from using the e-meter to come to terms with engrams, Scientologists use what they call "assists" – various techniques to relieve pain or discomfort. Light touch and mind distraction can constitute assists. Vitamins are also an important part of healthcare within Scientology. This is connected to both the Purification Rundown for ordinary Scientologists, and the drug detoxification program practiced at Narconon treatment facilities for drug users (Westbrook, 2022). Vitamins combined with exercise and nutritious foods are believed to clear many of the minor discomforts that people, including children, experience. Research with children of Scientologists in Sweden (which was by no means representative due to the small number) revealed that medication was exchanged for assist techniques and a "healthy" lifestyle (Frisk et al., 2018).

## Healthcare and Religious Faith

Sometimes in cases relating to health and medical treatment, the state's right to protect children is set against parents' rights of religious freedom. Monica Miller's article "Parents' Use of Faith Healing for their Children" (2016) addresses the question of how these two rights collide under the American constitution. While the First Amendment's Free Exercise Clause declares that the state may not prohibit the free exercise of religion, at the same time exceptions to the US Constitution have been made. According to the Supreme Court, exceptions may include prohibiting child labor and polygamy (Miller, 2016, p. 228). Christian Science is one new religious movement that has been harshly criticized due to its rejection of conventional medical treatment. It has, instead, practiced faith healing, and in some cases children have died from diseases that the medical community could have, according to current medical practice, cured. These illnesses include meningitis, obstructed bowels, and pneumonia. Although Christian Science practices have been questioned throughout the movement's history, legal judgments against members have become more frequent since 1980. Convictions involving involuntary manslaughter, felony child abuse, or child endangerment have resulted from the Christian Science belief that illness is the result of lack of faith and can therefore be cured by prayer.

A common feature of many new religious movements is that physical health is dependent on, or at least informed by, the amount of faith of the believer. This could result in members, and even children, blaming themselves for their illness. In my study of the children and youth in the Swedish Knutby Filadelfia congregation, some of those interviewed stated that they had felt personally responsible and criticized by their peers and adult members when they fell ill, as physical illness was definitely a sign of lack of faith or purity. In Daniel Lutz's autobiography on growing up in ISKCON, the author describes how his behavior as a child – being unable to sit still for long periods of time in class and the inability to concentrate – was attributed to his "bad karma." As an adult, he recognized the behavior as what would later be diagnosed as ADHD paired with response to trauma.

As we have seen in this section, behavior stemming from health issues is sometimes attributed to lack of faith on an individual level, while the same symptoms (for instance, those of ADHD) can be attributed to the use of psychiatric drugs. Moreover, in yet a third instance, they may indicate a heightened level of spirituality.

## 6 Custody and Abuse: Case Studies

This section examines claims of child abuse in new religious movements. It provides examples of allegations of physical and sexual abuse as well as abuse involved in custody cases. Allegations of abuse may come from former members, members of the public, and/or the media and have sometimes caused profound changes within the groups, such as fear of authorities, frequent relocation, and further isolation and/or aversion toward mainstream society.

Often claims of child abuse are connected to custody battles. Children might have one parent who is a member of a new religious movement while the other one is a former member or was never a member at all. In these cases, custody battles may involve the question of the child's rights regarding a parent's religion. One example comes from a custody case involving the Exclusive Brethren in Australia. One of the parents had left the group, and the remaining parent sought to restrict the other's visitation rights because they feared that the defector might "subject the child to different views in contravention with the Exclusive Brethren" (van Eck Duymaer van Twist, 2015, p. 180). Other custody battles have prompted state authorities to intervene on a larger scale, especially when the parent outside of the group has claimed that abuse is taking place. On the presumption that abuse might be widespread in a certain group, legal authorities have justified raiding different new religious movements on the grounds that they are rescuing the children. However, while it is necessary to immediately remove children from dangerous situations, it may not be necessary, or legal, to eliminate parental custody of all group members.

Another important aspect regarding accusations of abuse is the influence of the anticult movement. In both the cases of Peoples Temple and the Branch Davidians, former members and concerned relatives had come in contact with representatives of the anticult movement; some scholars argue that they influenced the actions taken by government authorities in Jonestown, Guyana (Hall et al., 2000) and in Waco, Texas (Tabor & Gallagher, 1995). These two examples of mass death have influenced the view that all new religious movements are prone to extreme physical and even deadly violence. However, my own research on children and youth in Knutby Filadelfia reveals that only the adults of the inner core membership suffered physical violence. Yet, my analysis also shows that the response by the wider community caused the group to increase isolation as well as the incidence of psychological violence, especially in the manifestation of social exclusion or *spiritual shunning*. This had profound effects on the relations between the teenagers in Knutby.

It is clear that, at particular times and particular places, physical and emotional abuse has been inflicted on children in new religious movements. This section examines the accusations against, and the responses by, the following groups: ISKCON, COG/TFI, The Twelve Tribes of Israel, Peoples Temple, the Branch Davidians, and the Knutby Filadelifa community. What becomes apparent in this overview is that each group is unique.

## ISKCON

At a meeting in Florida in 1996, several former gurukula students gathered to tell the leaders of ISKCON in North America about their experiences of abuse in the movement's schools. After that meeting, the grassroots organization Children of Krishna was formed, whose initiators and members were former gurukula students who gathered to support each other. In 1997, ISKCON started its first child protection work internationally, through the Task Force on Child Abuse in ISKCON. On the task force recommendation, the ISKCON Central Office of Child Protection was established; in March 1998, it was incorporated into the Association for the Protection of Vaishnava Children (Burt, 2023). In 2005, the association produced a policy document on how to deal with allegations of child abuse with clear guidelines. In 2009, the CPO was moved from the United States to South Africa but has been located in England since 2016 (Child Protection Office, 2018).

The CPO works with all ISKCON temples and recommends that all ISKCON centers have a child protection team responsible for child safety. The team should consist of two, three, or more members chosen by the members of the temple community – if it is a married couple, the lower limit is three. According to the policy documents, the ideal setup is that the group includes at least one parent, one teacher, and one ISKCON administrator. The child protection team must be well acquainted with ISKCON's policy regarding child safety and local laws and procedures when there is a suspicion of abuse. They must also ensure that adequate professional help is provided to the vulnerable. The CPO thus helps and trains the various child protection groups, which in turn train and inform the other members of the group and in some cases the children. The Child Protection Office also serves as an institution that child protection teams can turn to when a new member wants to move into an ISKCON community. Through a screening process, the child protection teams can request information on whether the member is on an internal list of suspected and/or convicted criminals who are members of ISKCON. The CPO can also give advice on how the person should be treated. All child protection teams are required to report all cases of abuse to the CPO, which then documents the information in its archives. The reason for this is that criminals should not be able to move between different temples or centers where their crimes may not be known, a problem that has previously existed (Wolf, 2004).

Unfortunately, the ISKCON CPO's funding was reduced by 97 percent between 1998 and 2021: from $150,000 to $5,000. There have been examples of known abusers participating in festivals and temple community activities with none of the attending parents having any idea that a sex offender is among them. A closer look at the documents outlining the judgments against offenders reveals a rhetoric that has little to do with protection from a child's perspective. In almost all cases, the judgments – made within ISKCON rather than by independent authorities – provide only a limited time of suspension from engaging in the activities of the temple community. In some cases, the conditions to reenter the temple center range from having to show the ruling of the CPO to the temple president, to being forbidden to stay overnight, or facing specific restrictions against giving class or leading kirtan, to writing letters of apology to the victims. In many cases, an additional condition is given: "NN cannot visit ISKCON property or attend an ISKCON function if the child sexual abuse victim or his/ her family members are present, *unless uncoerced and without manipulation, they give their consent*" (Padmapani Das, 2000). This condition is interesting. First, not all victims of abuse welcome receiving letters from their abusers. Second, the responsibility of being the one who must decide that a certain person is not welcome into the temple weighs heavy on many victims' shoulders, especially since the movement has a very clear hierarchical structure. In a more recent ruling, the ban on former guru Bhakti Vidya Purna, the sentence has changed, placing the responsibility of removing himself from the situation on the accused (ISKCON Communications, 2022). Since 2019, a grassroots movement headed by former gurukulis has lobbied to prevent known offenders from retaining high positions and/or reentering the movement without information being given to members. In 2022, prominent guru Bhakti Vidya Purna was excommunicated from his position at the Mayapura gurukula for having subjected children in his care to abuse and having not interfered when other high-ranking members did so. The debate started by the second-generation-led grassroots movement is now having a serious impact on a schism between Western and Indian factions within the organization. Together with opposing views on the possibility of female gurus, and "westernized" Krishna communities (see Burt, 2023), the question of children's rights and protection is increasingly dividing the movement.

## Children of God/The Family International

The group COG/TFI started out as a celibate organization and considered sex outside of marriage to be impure. This notion shifted to the understanding that denying another member sex was impure, as members were supposed to share love, including physical, with all members of the community. Similarly, varying expectations were placed on different generations of children. The first generation was subjected to extensive experimentation with sexuality and disciplining styles, which were sometimes inconsistent due to the order of certain leaders, individual interpretations of the teachings, and sometimes just certain adults' whims and wishes. Later generations were not as harshly disciplined. Because purity can sometimes serve as a ground for social relationships within religious systems, the comparison of ideas of purity within and between religious movements is fruitful for an analysis that highlights changing social boundaries.

In COG/TFI, the boundaries changed for several different reasons. One important aspect was state interventions, coming partly from accusations from anticult groups, from former members' statements, and critical media coverage. A notorious custody case in the 1990s, known as the Lord Justice Ward case, led the movement to compose a policy document detailing the new requirements of membership, which included prohibitions on sexual relations between adults, young adults, and children. Transgression would lead to excommunication. The composition and institution of the policy document, called The Charter, stemmed from the negative outcome of several interviews with youths of the group detailing harsh disciplinary punishment that had taken place in the group's resocialization training camps for teenagers (Borowick, 2023). While it became clear during the three-year-long custody case that there had been some serious abusive and even criminal practices going on, the judge ruled in favor of the mother who was still a member of The Family International, contending that while there was still improvement to be made in the group, they were on the right path (Ward, 1995).

## The Twelve Tribes of Israel

A group whose norms concerning child-rearing has been criticized as constituting child abuse is the Twelve Tribes of Israel. Also known simply as the Twelve Tribes, the group was founded in 1972 by Eugene and Marsha Spriggs in Chattanooga, Tennessee. Growing out of the Jesus Movement, and having broken off from the Presbyterian Church of Chattanooga in 1975, the group rejected mainstream Christianity because members wanted to live together as did the first-century church described in the New Testament. Through the years, the movement has had several names and has developed a specific theology rooted in Jewish and Christian faith that recognizes and anticipates the Second Coming of Christ while simultaneously reestablishing "ancient Jewish practice." Members adopt Jewish names, use the Jewish name Yahshua for Jesus, and have developed their own music and accompanying style of congregational dance. Members live in monogamous, heterosexual marriages within agricultural communes, produce and sell crops, handicrafts, and run health food bakeries and delicatessens. Children are homeschooled and make up almost half of the communities' members (Asadi, 2013). Children have a special role in the theology as it is believed that they constitute the people who are raised in preparation of the return of the Christ. One of the main aims of the community is to raise its children to be prepared to take on special roles in the coming world. Children are generally physically close to the adults as they participate in the work and activities of the community. Frisk writes that children have few toys and mostly use everyday items when playing, but that Lego blocks, jigsaw puzzles, and sewing kits as well as pens, paper, and wooden building blocks are used. Playing instruments and dancing constitutes a vital part of children's lives, as well as games where children and adults play together (Frisk, 2018c).

Twelve Tribes communities around the world have been raided more than once due to reports of child abuse. Like several of the movements described in this Element, the group (at that time called the Vine Community) was criticized by former members and parents of members. Between 1975 and 1978, they turned to the infamous anticult deprogrammer Ted Patrick of FREECOG to try to kidnap and deprogram eight members to leave the group (Palmer, 2010).

Having had problems with the anticult movement in Chattanooga, the community moved to Vermont where they went under the name Northeast Kingdom Community Church. In 1984, 112 children were taken into protective custody by Vermont State Police and social services from the group's community at Island Pond. This was the last in a series of events in which locals vandalized the community's properties and shot at members from vehicles. According to Palmer, a court ordered that the children be returned that night and the incident was deemed by authorities to have been excessive and harsh, since no signs of child abuse were found. The intervention made the leaders of the movement reconsider the value of cooperation with local society rather than isolation and Palmer stresses that as a consequence, several compromises between the authorities and the community ensued. One example is that the community was no longer obliged to list the names of the children in their care that were being homeschooled, but rather educational authorities were invited to visit the school and see the children. An officially recognized homeschool program was approved by the Vermont Department of Education in 1990 (Palmer, 2010). The community has since interpreted the raid at Island Pond to have spiritual significance.

Children in the Twelve Tribes are raised to be obedient and respectful of their elders, as adults believe that the third or fourth generation of children in their communities will be among the 144,000 stated in the Book of Revelation to be the ones to usher in the millennium (Palmer, 2010). In order to raise obedient and God-fearing children, an important part of child-rearing is the biblical decree not to "spare the rod" (Proverbs 13:24). This discipline, using a flexible plastic rod, is administered to children up to the age of twelve and can be carried out by a parent or another appointed adult member of the community. The group stresses that physical disciplining is an act of love and guidance, not an act of frustration with a disobedient child. The original guidelines for child disciplining were given by Eugene Spiggs. One standard states that spanking should be carried out in a controlled manner and leave no marks on the body; thus, it aligned with contemporary law when the practice was adopted.

In the twenty-first century, Twelve Tribes communities are spread over the globe. There are farms in different parts of Europe and North America. In 2013, the police in Germany raided a Twelve Tribes community in Bavaria, taking forty children and adolescents ranging in age from seventeen months to seventeen years into protective custody after allegations of child abuse. The raid was prompted by the publication of a short video sequence where mothers are seen administering corporal punishment to children in the community. The footage was aired after a German news reporter had infiltrated the community, posing as a possible convert. While the children had been returned immediately in the case of the raid on Island Pond in 1984, the raid in Germany resulted in several of the children being put into foster care, some for several months; some children tried to return home by running away from foster care. When the children were medically examined, doctors found no evidence of abuse and most children could return to their parents. The raid, however, prompted several families to leave Germany and migrate to the Czech Republic, where they felt that the rights of parents to socialize children in accordance with religious belief was protected (Frisk, 2018c).

## Peoples Temple

An example of a tragic as well as complex event in which custody issues and child abuse played a role are the mass murders–suicides of Peoples Temple in Jonestown, Guyana in 1978, where more than 900 people died in an act defined by the charismatic leader Jim Jones as "revolutionary suicide" (Moore, 2006). Although referred to as mass suicide, implying a voluntary collective decision and act, some survivors are more likely to refer to it as murder, since children had no choice in the matter and some members were forcibly injected with poison (Carter, 2006).

Founded in Indianapolis in the 1950s, Peoples Temple distinguished itself through the incorporation of socialist values into its Christian base. Charity directed at the local community was an important part of its practice as were church services and attending to the elders of the congregation. The group, with Jones and his wife Marceline as its leaders, was especially notable for their fight for the integration of races in a time when racial segregation was the norm. The congregation relocated from Indianapolis to California in 1965, where Jones began to emerge more clearly to his members as a charismatic leader, identifying himself as a prophet of God. A new practice, termed "catharsis," in which members were to confess their sins and were sometimes subjected to corporal punishment, was instituted around this time. By 1976, Jones had become a visible political figure in San Francisco and members of Peoples Temple were involved in several campaigns to end segregation, inviting important political and cultural personalities to speak in their church. Meanwhile, abusive practices within the church became public when defectors spoke out about them. Driven by a vision to create an agricultural village as a place to escape the racism of America, Temple members in 1974 began building what would become known as "Jonestown." By the end of 1977, the vision of a utopian community had prompted almost a thousand members to move to Guyana. But a group of relatives, organizing under the name Concerned Relatives, took their worries over the well-being of their family members to the media. Demanding government attention, the Concerned Relatives found an ally in Congressman Leo J. Ryan, who had taken an interest in the group. Former Temple leaders Grace and Tim Stoen contacted Ryan to ask for help in a custody case concerning their six-year-old son John Victor Stoen, who lived in Guyana with Jim Jones (Moore, 2022).

The custody case of John Victor Stoen served as a triggering event for the mass murders–suicides, according to religious studies scholar Rebecca Moore (2022). In 1972, Tim Stoen had signed an affidavit stating that John Victor was the child of Jim Jones and Stoen's wife Grace. Jim and his wife Marceline had several adopted children, but the initial reason as to why the affidavit was signed is not fully clear. John Victor was raised by the community in Jonestown, having little to no contact with his mother Grace when she decided to leave the community in 1976. Tim Stoen left the community early in 1977 and later that year the couple embarked upon a mission to regain custody of John Victor. Although a California judge ruled in Grace and Tim's favor, Jim Jones refused to hand John Victor over to them, claiming that he was the biological father of John Victor. The situation was stressful not only for Jim Jones but also for the entire Jonestown community. If John Victor was returned to his parents, Jones would have betrayed a promise he had given to always take care of the members. This could have resulted in decreasing power and, Moore argues, the fear that additional custody issues would force other children in the group to return to the United States (Moore, 2022). The community had several foster children and was not willing to relinquish them. The importance of John Victor's case was confirmed by a defector, leaving Jonestown about six months before the arrival of Stoen's parents with congressman Leo Ryan. Debbie Layton Blakey then told the staff at the embassy in Georgetown, Guyana that "the loss of John Victor Stoen by Jim Jones would push Jones to force all of Jonestown to commit suicide" (Yates, 2020).

In addition to custody issues, the Concerned Relatives also raised issues of child abuse, and there were indeed acts of abuse occurring. The members of the congregation had been subjected to physical punishment during disciplining sessions, taking place behind closed doors. The general idea was to socialize members in what Jones considered socialist values. Children also were the targets of the behavioral modification, known as catharsis. The sessions of catharsis typically included calling members out "on the floor" where they would be criticized by Jones and fellow members until they admitted to their supposed misdeeds. Initially, the sessions consisted of exhausting hours of chastising, but by 1972, they came to include physical punishments as well. Former members recounted how up to 100 members would be lined up to be beaten with a wooden paddle or ordered into staged boxing matches with their fellow members, beaten with belts and severely spanked in front of the whole congregation. The social control and humiliation aspects in the catharsis sessions are most evident in cases where members were ordered to write incriminating letters where they would confess to made-up criminal deeds. Other examples of socialization through punishment included intense work around the church for those considered lazy (Moore, 2022).

As stated earlier, children also participated in catharsis. Children were, for instance, bitten back if they had bitten someone. One teenage girl was beaten seventy-five times with a stick because she had hugged and kissed a female friend who was reputed to be a lesbian. Other instances of abuse of children are detailed in Kenneth Wooden's book *The Children of Jonestown* (1981). Apart from being disciplined physically in the family gatherings during catharsis, some of the children and youth were subjected to psychological abuse through acts of terror when they were living in Jonestown. For instance, adults would take a child to a nearby hole where the child was blindfolded and made to believe that snakes and monsters were attacking them. Children and youth could be locked in a small plywood box for a day or more until they repented their misbehavior. One boy recounted how he got his teeth knocked out and others reported that they had to work endless hours or be cramped in together in a small cottage (Wooden, 1981, pp. 6–11). Children as well as adults were "sent out to the tiger," a practice in which children would be tied to a tree and left out in the jungle while adults made scary noises (Moore, 2022, p. 41).

When, in November 1978, Congressman Ryan decided to investigate Jonestown, his visit fit well into the already existing conspiracy theory and persecution narrative preached by Jones. Residents had moved to Guyana to live in peace without the intrusion of authorities, yet, here was a member of the U.S. Congress, flying out to scrutinize their community. Arriving with Ryan were the Stoens, people from the Concerned Relatives, other former members who had filed lawsuits against Jim Jones, and reporters who had written critically about Jones and Jonestown. Moore (2022) states that although the group had been preparing for a mass suicide through rehearsals, the visit – invasion, in their words – of perceived enemies may well have precipitated the events that led to the deaths of more than 300 children. At the time of the deaths, Jim Jones recorded the event on a tape that indicates that not everyone was willing to kill the children for the sake of the cause. A woman named Christine Miller takes the floor and asks Jones if there's not a chance that they could go to Russia. She is opposing the inclusion of the children in what Jones has planned for them. She states that she is not afraid to die herself but says: "But I look at all the babies and I think they deserve to live" (FBI Audiotape Q042, 1978). Jones's rhetoric when he dismisses her claims that the children be saved is particularly interesting and illustrates the role of the children's perceived future in the narrative. Jones tells Miller that it is better that they "lay down their lives" for if they don't, the antagonists will destroy the children's lives, implying that the threat from outside has consequences perhaps even beyond this life. Jones continues, "I don't think we should sit here and take any more time for our children to be endangered, for if they come after our children and we give them our children, then our children will suffer forever" (FBI Audiotape Q042, 1978). He goes on to say that when the authorities come there, they will torture the children and elders, trying thereby to speed up the process of killing. When the smallest children are given the poison, an unidentified woman tells the older children to reassure the smaller ones and guarantees that the children are not crying from pain but from the bitter taste of the poison. Adult members are crying and the small children continue screaming and crying, and even when an unidentified speaker tells of how he's glad to see the children lying dead rather than having to grow up "to become dummies," children's shrill screams can be heard. Jones repeatedly asks the children to calm down, but he is also chastising the adults for "exciting the children" by telling them that they are dying. Adults telling the children to stop crying can be heard several times throughout the tape until, after forty-five minutes, all falls silent.

## The Branch Davidians

Charges of child abuse led to the storming of the Branch Davidian residence at Mount Carmel near Waco, Texas in 1993. Former group members persuaded law-enforcement officials that minors were being abused. The Davidian Seventh-day Adventist splinter group, the Branch Davidians, had created a community outside Waco. The group, headed by leader David Koresh (b. Vernon Howell 1959), was aiming to create what Koresh called the "House of David," a special people awaiting the impending end of the world. To achieve this goal, Koresh proclaimed that he was called by God to procreate with the women of the group, while men were required to observe celibacy. This involved Koresh having sexual intercourse with underage girls. The foundation of this practice was Koresh's teaching that his own offspring would be special children; he compared them to the twenty-four elders in Revelation 4:4.

While an investigation by the office of Texas Child Protective Services in 1992 found no evidence of abuse of any kind (Tabor & Gallagher, 1995, p. 101), a former member by the name of Marc Breault was convinced that at least one of the young girls was at risk of sexual abuse. He contacted her father, David Jewell, who was not a member of the Branch Davidians, and convinced him to take legal action to get his daughter out of the group. Breault testified in court that Koresh had, in 1989, announced himself as the sole male to be granted the right to have sexual relations with the women of the group, including teenage girls. Breault included in his testimony that physical child abuse as well as living conditions were unfit for minors and that Koresh was obsessed with guns. David Jewell was eventually granted joint custody of his daughter, Kiri. The mother, Sherrie Jewell, who still lived at Mount Carmel, was given visitation rights, as long as visitations took place outside of the group and did not involve Koresh. (Sherri Jewell never exercised this right and subsequently died in the FBI assault on the community on April 19, 1993.)

The custody case alerted the authorities to the possibility that Koresh was keeping illegal firearms at Mount Carmel. The Bureau of Alcohol, Tobacco, and Firearms (ATF) was already interested in the Branch Davidians because of an account from a United Parcel Service driver that a large number of grenades had been delivered to the group. The ATF contacted Breault ten weeks prior to the 1993 raid at Mount Carmel and the *Waco Herald Tribune* began to publish a series of articles called "The Sinful Messiah" only a few days before the beginning of the standoff in February 1993. The newspaper articles included allegations that Koresh had physically and sexually abused underage girls in the group. Both the newspaper articles and accounts of weapons that spurred the siege relied heavily on the expertise of an anticult group called the Cult Awareness Network and the testimonies of a small group of former members. Tabor and Gallagher highlight in their book *Why Waco?* (1995) how the "cult narrative" had a great impact on developments at Mount Carmel.

On February 28, 1993, the ATF attempted to serve a search warrant upon David Koresh, based on the agency's conviction that the group was guilty of weapons violations. On that day, an undercover agent from the ATF was revealed and left, reporting to his superiors that the Branch Davidians knew of the impending raid. Shortly thereafter, gunfire ensued, but it is unclear whether the first shots came from the agents outside the community or from inside the Davidian facility. Either way, a gunfight followed, which killed six group members and four ATF agents. When the ATF ran out of ammunition, they retreated, and the FBI took over the situation, which resulted in a fifty-one-day siege.

Four of the children in the community were escorted out by their parents on February 28. They were initially sent to the Methodist Children's Home in Waco. In the following days, a total of eighteen children left the Mount Carmel center in small groups. Most were taken to the children's home. Two were sent out together with two elderly ladies, carrying a tape that Koresh wanted to be played on radio. The two ladies were arrested but later released. The children were studied by Dr. Bruce Perry while in the children's home. Perry and Szlavitz's subsequent article, "Stairway to Heaven: Treating Children at the Crosshairs of Trauma," illustrates how the raid on the center was traumatizing for the children. Perry got to spend six weeks with the children, stating that Child Protective Services had tried to place them in individual foster homes but were unable to find as many as were needed, so the children were together for the first six weeks. This proved to be fortunate, as the children had been brought up to fear outsiders and would have been even more terrified had they been immediately separated from their siblings and peers. The article further concludes that although they grew up in the group, the children who were later sent to live with loving relatives fared better than those put in institutions. The article presents an important insight into the reality for children of raided religious communities. Perry stresses the point that members of the FBI may have had the best intentions, but in a situation like the one in Waco, they were too focused on solving the immediate problem and were initially not considering the fact that the children they wanted to question immediately after leaving the site of conflict were traumatized: not simply by being in the group but additionally by having been removed from their parents after witnessing members of the group being killed in the siege (Perry & Szlavitz, 2006, pp. 60–1).

Several adults were negotiated out up until March 23; some later faced criminal charges and had to serve time in prison (Doyle, 2012, p. 184). During the siege, the FBI used different tactics to try to get the members to leave the center. The electricity was cut off and high beam lights were directed at the building all through the night; loud music and disturbing sounds were played, which must have been scary for the smaller children. US Attorney General Janet Reno, basing her decision primarily on FBI reports that relied upon anticult rhetoric, believed that children were continuously being abused within the group and that there was a risk of mass suicide. She therefore approved, and even argued for, the final assault that led to the death of most members inside the facilities.

On the morning of April 19, the Branch Davidians were informed that the FBI would begin to insert CS gas into the building and were urged to surrender. Tanks were driven into the building, causing parts of the walls to collapse. Women and children were told by Branch Davidian leaders to go down into a concrete vault, which was believed to be a safer space; however, it was later revealed that gas had been directly sprayed into the vault. As there was no ventilation, the gas quickly killed those sheltering in a virtual death trap (Doyle, 2012, p. 149). After a few hours, the entire building caught fire, killing seventy-six members, including twenty-two children under the age of thirteen (two infants were born as their mothers died). The source of the fire is disputed; the FBI claims that the Branch Davidians started it, while former members and several experts believe that it was deliberately or accidently started through the actions of the FBI. Either way, only three women and six men survived it.

## The Fundamentalist Church of Latter-Day Saints

Another instance of child abuse claims leading to government action against a new religion occurred in 2008. The Fundamentalist Church of Latter-Day Saints (FLDS) community Yearning for Zion ranch in El Dorado, Texas, a community of approximately 800 members, was raided on April 3. The FLDS is a Mormon sect that split from the major church in 1952; in the twenty-first century, members were living in their own communities, practicing polygamy under the charismatic leader Warren Jeffs (b. 1955). What prompted the raid was a phone call to a domestic violence shelter purporting to be from a teenage member who claimed that her much older husband was violently abusing her. Although the girl had given her own name and the name of her husband, the state police were unable to find them in the community. Despite this fact, the Texas Rangers and other officials took 439 children and youth – the entire population of minors – into state custody. No previous custodial detention of this scale had been carried out in the history of the United States. The children were removed from the ranch and the mothers were given the choice of either going to a shelter for domestic violence or returning to the ranch – however, those who chose to return were told they would not be seeing their children again (Goodwin, 2018, p. 249).

It was later revealed that the call for rescue had been a prank call by a mentally disturbed thirty-three-year-old woman, previously convicted of similar instances of false calls about sexual abuse (Wright & Richardson, 2011). It also turned out that twenty-nine of those taken into custody were adult women who had been mistaken for minors. There was, however, a handful of pubescent girls between the ages of fifteen to seventeen found to have had babies (Schreinert & Richardson, 2011, p. 258). Consequently, ten men, including Warren Jeffs, were arrested, tried, and convicted of abusing or facilitating abuse of underage girls (Goodwin, 2018, p. 250).

The impact of apostates (former members who publicly denounced the group), anticult activists, and the media in the case of the FLDS is highlighted by Wright and Fagen (2011) in a comparison with the case of the Branch Davidians. The interesting part of their study is that the claims against the groups include – in addition to child abuse and polygamy as well as underage marriage – features such as brainwashing, mass suicide, and "another Jonestown" (Wright & Fagen, 2011, p. 154). The claim that the groups were at risk of becoming another Jonestown is clearly problematic, as in both cases it had a great impact on the development of the raids, which might otherwise have been carried out in a fashion less intimidating, or indeed traumatizing, for the children of the groups.

Richardson and Schreinert (2011) compare the intervention by state authorities in this case with the investigations into abuse of children within the Catholic Church. They observe that there are great differences between a SWAT team storming the community of FLDS and the institutional introspection that occurred over a long period of time in the case of abuses reported in the Catholic Church. They argue that the most troubling aspect of the use of government raids to remove children from religious minorities is that this way of handling the potential threats of abuse prevents the possibility for actual abuse victims in the groups to make themselves heard; they are often afraid of the harsh treatment by the authorities. This is further confirmed by defectors of FLDS and other communities with similar experiences (Richardson & Shreinert, 2011, pp. 232–5).

## The Knutby Filadelfia Congregation

Sweden has not experienced religious violence in relation to new religious movements on the scale of Jonestown or Waco. In fact, large-scale violence connected to religious ideas is altogether uncommon. Nevertheless, when the 2004 murder of Alexandra Fossmo in the Knutby Filadelfia congregation was exposed, self-proclaimed cult expert and minister in the Church of Sweden Karl-Erik Nylund immediately drew parallels to the fates of the Peoples Temple and the Branch Davidians, stating that the congregation's refusal to accept help from the Pentecostal movement was a sign of impending catastrophe. Backed by the anticult movement and so-called atrocity tales coming from former members and parents of members, the fear of mass suicide influenced reporting about the groups. The comparison aggravated the members, and the congregation closed its ranks to outsiders. The close connection between representatives of the anticult movement, former members, and the mass media is well-known among scholars of new religious movements (Hall et al., 2000, p. 72). Sometimes, this can be seen in the presence of a metanarrative unintentionally generated by former group members about experiences within the group.

Ex-members may strive toward conformity with their new identity as a defector among other defectors. Because of the relatively small size of Knutby Filadelfia, the defectors were few. Nevertheless, they were cited in media, and so a metanarrative of abuse and hardship was constructed. Moreover, the same defector could be cited under diverse pseudonyms, which may have expanded the metanarrative, as it would seem to involve more former members than was actually the case. However, one must be careful not to equate metanarratives with false testimonies. Bromley and Shupe (1979) termed the phenomenon of defectors' stories *atrocity tales*, defining them as symbolic presentations of actions or events, real or imaginary, in such a way as to "(a) evoke moral outrage by specifying and detailing the value violations (b) authorize implicitly or explicitly, punitive sanctions, and (c) mobilize control efforts against the perceived perpetrators" (Bromley & Shupe, 1979, p. 43). While the definition in itself is applicable, I find the term "metanarrative" more useful in this context as it denotes a less calculated and pejorative overarching story that serves to give totalizing meaning to different events, including historical, social, and cultural phenomena based on a perceived universal truth. Since no academic research has been conducted regarding the construction of a metanarrative in defectors from the Knutby Filadelfia congregation, it is not possible at this point to validate the accuracy of this hypothesis in this particular case.

Knutby Filadelfia was founded in 1921 as a Pentecostal congregation. It operated as a part of the independent Pentecostal groups in Sweden up until Pastor Kim Wincent came to Knutby in 1985. Wincent had been attending Bible school at the Word of Life, a growing charismatic congregation in Sweden that attracted several thousands of new members. The Word of Life congregation was seen as controversial, being influenced by the Faith Movement. Wincent brought back charismatic influences, including the focus on prophecies, glossolalia, healing, and evil spirits, to the congregation in Knutby. By the time that Pastor Åsa Waldau, who was to become the charismatic leader known to outsiders as The Bride of Christ, came to Knutby in 1992, the congregation was already moving away from traditional Pentecostalism. Both Wincent and Waldau were strong leaders who managed to engage the members, and the congregation that had been quite small started to grow, partly because of the Bible training schools that Waldau initiated. In 1997, another pastor, Helge Fossmo, moved to Knutby with his wife. Waldau and Fossmo became a well-known team throughout the Swedish Pentecostal milieu and they managed to invite several young Pentecostals to join the congregation in Knutby where the membership increased. However, the influences from the charismatic movement were not welcomed by all members of the Pentecostal milieu. Fossmo and Waldau started to perform healing sessions bordering on exorcisms and were asked by some congregations not to return. However, those who did come to Knutby to stay became more and more convinced that the leadership in their particular congregation was special, something that was theologically at odds with the democratic structure of

Pentecostalism. The teachings in Knutby were focusing more and more on the prophecies of the leadership, one of which preceded the death of Helge Fossmo's wife Helene, which he told a few members about.

When Helene Fossmo died in 1999, it seemed to prove to the members of the congregation that Helge had indeed been able to foresee the future by prophecy. That same year, Åsa Waldau and Helge Fossmo claimed that Åsa was wed to Jesus and announced to core members that she was the Bride of Christ. It follows that the sacred mandate was in place, namely the important part that Åsa Waldau would play in the transformative events. The events to come would ultimately lead to the destruction of the existing social order, which would bring about another, purer existence. In this new narrative, the youth group, formed several years later by the leaders' children who were still small at that time, came to hold a special position. When it came into being, the adult leaders called it The Horse, hinting that the young ones were wild horses galloping into the kingdom of God, while the older ones, their parents, were not energetic enough. Furthermore, since the doctrine of the Bride of Christ was not questioned, it created a self-sealing thought system in which criticism was met with congregational disciplining. Defectors testify to the collective psychological exclusion of members who dared question Åsa Waldau and her revelation. Inclusion was only possible when Åsa had decided that the time was right or that the member had repented sufficiently.

The gradual withdrawal from other Pentecostal congregations may have also contributed to an increasing emphasis on the congregation, and specifically of Åsa Waldau, as chosen for a special purpose. When I interviewed children and youth in the beginning of 2014, I soon spotted a pattern of what I termed a *grand narrative of persecution* within the group (Nilsson, 2019). As with other new religious movements, pressure from outsiders and the media had created (or perhaps enhanced) an antagonistic situation in which group members felt persecuted and misunderstood. They expressed sadness and anger that their leader had been especially targeted by the media, although the murder victim had been her sister. The distrust in surrounding society was clearly evident, and youth members had practically grown up in the marginalization of Sweden's most notorious "cult." The persecution narrative fit well into the theology that put Åsa Waldau in the center as the Bride of Christ, since it additionally included a notion of how she sacrificed her own privacy, happiness, and life in order to protect the congregation. She, as well as the members, maintained that she took all the criticism upon her while she protected the congregation from the attacks from outsiders.

It seems probable that not all members of the congregation held the esoteric belief that Åsa Waldau was the Bride of Christ, but there was clearly the idea of

Åsa being pure and several of the adolescents belonging to the youth group knew her exalted status before their parents did. This information was only available to a chosen few. The remaining members may have understood Åsa Waldau as having a closer connection to Jesus, but not necessarily that she had been betrothed to him in a ceremony or was expecting to rule by his side. In Knutby Filadelfia, the youth group in time came to be part of the decision-making inner group. The members of the youth group were made up of sixteen to twenty young members, ranging in age between twelve and twenty-five. While the younger children of the congregation socialized mostly with the children of the families living nearby (or together with) themselves, the members of the youth group formed a tight-knit group led by Åsa Waldau's children. While her son took seriously his role as a leader of the boys of the youth group, her daughter, who was two years older, was less interested in the role given to her. As an illustration of the impact of the youth leaders, my adult gatekeeper (who was also a pastor in the congregation) felt that he had to get permission from the then-sixteen-year-old son of Åsa Waldau, to conduct my interviews. Observations with the youth group confirmed the power of its leaders. When they gathered to plan an upcoming summer camp for the younger children, the leaders of the youth group were clearly in charge, their opinions sometimes more valued than the other pastors. At the time, there were three male pastors, in addition to Åsa Waldau.

One young man, Urban Fält, had joined the congregation and came to replace Fossmo by Waldau's side. As Waldau increasingly withdrew from the congregation in 2008, only associating with members of the inner circle and the youth group, Fält acted as a middle management person between her and the congregation. Fält's charisma was enhanced by his rock star looks and the fact that he was lead singer in the congregation's own band. However, when a secret relationship with a seventeen-year-old girl was revealed, along with the fact that a few adult members also had sexual relations with Fält, he was kicked out. (The teen who had been involved with Fält confessed to her parents, which led to a conflict between her and Åsa Waldau, who was later convicted of physically assaulting the teenager by jumping on her ribs until they fractured.) A few weeks after Fält's expulsion, Waldau was also ordered to leave the congregation. One of the remaining leaders went to the police to hand himself over, stating that he had physically abused another man in the congregation. This led to a long investigation and subsequent trial of the leaders of the group. Former pastors Peter Gembäck, Urban Fält, and Åsa Waldau were convicted in 2020 of minor assault, sexual exploitation of a dependent person, and assault, respectively. Over the previous four to six years, the inner core circle had gotten increasingly isolated from the remaining congregation. Waldau's demands on them to show 100 percent loyalty had taken on the form of ordering them to physically discipline each other.

While the members of the youth group did not resort to that form of physical violence, the increasingly heightened tension in the core group of adults spilled over to them, which resulted in psychological punishments and outright bullying. When the adult core group assembled on Saturday nights in Åsa Waldau's house, the youth group would have a similar Saturday night dinner of their own. As with the adult group, the leaders' children would decide if one of the other youths had behaved in a bad way, weren't "standing right" with one of the youth leaders, or had in some way misbehaved. In the adult group, Waldau decided who was to be shunned and excluded, and in the youth group, her children were expected to do the same. If someone failed to show up on the Saturday night dinner, the others would know that person was in spiritual shunning, social exclusion. There could otherwise be a conversation led by the youth leaders in which one particular youth would be targeted by the others, who insisted that (s)he had committed one sin or another. As no one wanted to be put in that position, the drive to be close to the leaders of the youth group led to internal conflicts. Copying the behavior of the adults, several of the other youth of the youth group chastised their own parents, if they were not members of the core group, as they chastised each other. The seventeen-year-old girl was particularly targeted although none of the youth were aware of the reason until knowledge of the abuse by Fält finally broke a circle of violence that was threatening the group's very existence. Another girl whose mother had been spiritually shunned by Åsa Waldau for several years was ordered to move to the Waldau house and permitted to see her own parents only once a week. Since the mother was shunned (and the father of the family was unaware), the power balance in that family was altered. The teenage girl was understood to be standing much closer to Åsa Waldau and thereby to God, while her mother was deemed impure and lost.

The dynamics of these relations are portrayed in her autobiographical book *The Knutby Girl* (2020) where she further details her life and the forced friendship, as she understood it, between herself and the Waldau children. When Fält and then Åsa Waldau were forced to leave in 2016, several of the members of the youth group, including the leaders, came forward with their stories of growing up inside Knutby Filadelfia. One story in particular is that of Åsa Waldau's daughter, who described her longing for an ordinary family life, how she detested being designated the role of leader, and how she took to the fictive worlds of computer games to interact with peers her own age online who were unaware that she was the daughter of "The Bride of Christ" (Nilsson, 2023). Knutby Filadelfia officially dissolved in 2018 and many of the youth have since become parents and assumed careers that would not have been within their reach while members of the congregation.

As illustrated by these examples, understanding abuse of children within new religions is complex. Although some general similarities can be outlined, each group has a unique set of beliefs that develop differently and that impact the occurrence of abuse in the form of legitimizing the treatment through a theological perspective. As most of the groups are organized around one or a few charismatic leaders, who may claim prophetic gifts, the content of the religious belief is dynamic and prone to rapid change. Many leaders, as we have seen, put special emphasis on the role of the children: They will fulfill the religious duties that their parents were unable to. Sometimes this leads to a reversed relation of authority between biological parents and children, and sometimes to separation. Both developments increase the risk of the parent lacking the information, courage, or even the possibility of protecting the child from abuse. Sometimes abuse is disguised as religious practice, which can result in conflicting emotions for the child: positive for being selected, negative for going against their inner will.

## 7 Concluding Observations

This Element has aimed at illustrating the great variety of childhoods experienced within the groups that we call new religious movements as well as the sometimes polemical differences in perspectives on researching these childhoods. Critiques of these groups at times portray them as intrinsically dangerous environments for children and conclude that parents who, for instance, give their children up for others in the religious group to raise must be brainwashed into doing so. However, while there are indeed cases where parents have in hindsight regretted parting with their children on the orders of a charismatic leader, there are also parents and former child members who recognize some value in growing up in a close-knit group with nonbiological parental caregivers. Just as historian Edward Shorter's conclusions about the modern family being based on love marriages as the sole institution where children were showed affection was criticized, so this Element would like to call into question the assumptions that parents who let their children be raised by others in new religious groups automatically do so against their own will or against their own best judgment. The dynamics within such groups differ from group to group, and within them over time, as does every parent–child relationship. We still lack the necessary number of long-term studies into these childhoods to make well-grounded analysis. What if the placement of a child within the care of the group is understood as a voluntary act of care? Or even a religious offering? Does such an understanding exist over time, regardless of the membership of children and parents, or is there a pattern to be seen in cohorts of parents and children who have left their religious group that differs from the cohort that stayed?

The contemporary discussion of children growing up in newer new religious movements can be analyzed through the lenses of the Apollonian versus Dionysian images of children (see Section 2). The Apollonian image saw children as a "vessel for parental idolization and almost worship," and the Dionysian image saw children as untamed and in need of restriction and rules. In the studies of children in new religious groups, we have seen that there are examples of the Apollonian images of childhood, such as in the case of the so-called blessed children – that is, children born into the movement who, in several cases, are given a very important role in the group's eschatology. In this image, children are seen as pure, as the only redeemers, and they thus become the subject of the adult members' veneration. Although it may benefit some children, this elevated status for others can become confusing as it affects the parent–child relationships by overturning authority. For some children, however, the responsibility of rescuing all humanity in the Endtime can create a sense of euphoria, which results in elitist thinking, sparking creativity, and elevating self-esteem; while to still others, it may invoke an alarming sense of pressure, leaving the child feeling shame because of his/her reluctance to assume the role of savior.

As has been highlighted in this Element, the focus on children in newer new religions rarely ventures beyond the scope of contested issues, such as abuse and neglect; meanwhile, data collected by research into the everyday life of these children is much needed. As has been discussed, new religious movements have a tendency of dissolving after the first or second generation, which means that new groups are continuously forming. When a certain movement is given public attention, it is most often initially by the media, which uses former members and/ or representatives of various anticult groups as sources. The media has little or no interest in everyday life but is often keen on a sensational cult story, so the news that is produced tends to revolve around problematic aspects (or perceived deviance) of a group. The interaction between the media and the anticult movement sometimes causes groups to live in hiding, making academic research into childhood even harder to access as members. Leaders especially are afraid of criticism, in particular when it comes to socialization methods and alleged abuse of children. As a result, it is difficult for researchers to obtain funding into children in new religions if the study does not focus on potential harm. Influenced by the overarching narrative that these groups are dangerous, funding agencies are unwilling to investigate the more controversial issue: How are children to be raised?

Due to the rapid process of globalization, ethnic groups, religious traditions, cultures, and customs are intersecting all over the world. One result of this is that different understandings of childhood, norms regarding the socialization of children, and children's role in the economic structure of the community are continuously negotiated. Some countries, for instance, forbid all physical punishment of children while others differentiate between corporal discipline and outright abuse (for instance, by laws regarding whether marks are left on the child's body). Some countries forbid homeschooling while others permit it, and there are different regulations regarding parental rights as well as the rights of children. One interesting aspect is the differing levels of understanding of children's participation in religious rituals, where highly individualized communities tend to emphasize the autonomy of the child and more traditional ones see the given roles of children within the religious practices as very important. The differences in understanding beliefs regarding socialization of children produce a variety of parenting models.

As has been argued in this Element, parenting styles in new religions offer a wide range of innovative approaches to socialization. Because of the reliance on prophecy, the groups' teachings tend to change more rapidly than beliefs in general and this too affects norms concerning children. The children themselves also affect the groups' beliefs, structures, and even survival at a pace that is uncommon in larger society. Case studies researching the parenting styles within these unusual groups therefore provide an opportunity to expand our understanding of community, parenting, and childhood in a way that is conducive to the overall study of children's religious lives.

# References

Åkerbäck, P. (2018). "Recently Reborn: To Return as a Child of Scientology Parents." In L. Frisk, S. Nilsson, & P. Åkerbäck (eds.), *Children in Minority Religions: Growing Up in Controversial Groups*, 97–121. Sheffield: Equinox.

Ariès, P. (1962). *Centuries of Childhood: A Social History of Family Life*. New York: Vintage Books.

Arnett, J. J. (2007). "Emerging Adulthood: What Is It, and What Is It Good for?" *Child Development Perspectives*, 1(2): 68–73. https://doi.org/10.1111/j.1750-8606.2007.00016.x

Asadi, T. (2013). "A Tradition of Innovation and the Innovation of Tradition: The Cultural Developments of the Twelve Tribes Community." In T. Miller (ed.), *Spiritual and Visionary Communities: Out to Save the World*, 139–56. London: Routledge.

Barker, E. (1984). *The Making of a Moonie: Choice or Brainwashing*. Oxford: Basil Blackwell.

Beckford, J. (1985). *Cult Controversies: The Societal Response to New Religious Movements*. London: Cambridge University Press.

Berger, P. L. & T. Luckmann. (1966). *The Social Construction of Reality: A Treatise in the Sociology of Knowledge*. Garden City, NY: Doubleday.

Bhaktivedanta, A. C. (2006). *Bhagavad Gita as It Is*. Alachua, FL: The Bhaktivedanta Book Trust.

Borowik, C. (2023). *From Radical Jesus People to Virtual Religion: The Family International*. Cambridge: Cambridge University Press.

Boswell, J. (1988). *The Kindness of Strangers: The Abandonment of Children in Western Europe from Late Antiquity to the Renaissance*. Chicago, IL: University of Chicago Press.

Bowers, B. (1989). *What Color Is Your Aura?: Personality Spectrums for Understanding and Growth*. New York: Pocket Books.

Bromley, D. G. (2011). "Dramatic Denouements." In D. G. Bromley & J. G. Melton (eds.), *Cults, Religion, and Violence*, 11–41. Cambridge: Cambridge University Press.

Bromley, D. G. & A. Shupe. (1979). "Atrocity Tales, the Unification Church, and the Social Construction of Evil." *Journal of Communication*, 29 (Summer): 42–53.

Bromley, D. G. & A. Shupe. (1987). "The Future of the Anti-cult Movement." In D. G. Bromley & P. Hammond (eds.), *The Future of New Religious Movements*, 224–34. Macon, GA: Mercer University Press.

Burt, A. R. (2023). *Hare Krishna in the Twenty-First Century.* Cambridge: Cambridge University Press.

Carroll, L. & J. Tober. (1998). *The Indigo Children: The New Kids Have Arrived.* Carlsbad, CA: Hay House.

Carter, T. (2006). "Murder or Suicide: What I Saw." Was It Murder or Suicide: A Forum. *The Jonestown Report* 8. https://jonestown.sdsu.edu/?page_id=31976

Chancellor, J. D. (2000). *Life in the Family. An Oral History of the Children of God.* Syracuse, NY: Syracuse University Press.

Chryssides, G. D. (2016). *Jehovah's Witnesses: Continuity and Change.* London: Ashgate.

Chryssides, G. D. (2019). *Historical Dictionary on the Jehovah's Witnesses,* 2nd ed. Lanham, MD: Rowman & Littlefield.

Cunningham, H. (2005). *Children and Childhood in Western Society since 1500.* London: Pearson.

Das, P. (2000). "Official Decision On Maha-Mantra Dasa." *Vaishnava News,* June 19. https://vaishnava-news-network.org/world/WD0006/WD19-6038.html

Delano, S. F. (2004). *Brook Farm: The Dark Side of Utopia.* Cambridge, MA: Belknap Press at Harvard University Press.

DeMause, L. (1974). *The History of Childhood.* Lanham, MD: Rowman & Littlefield.

Douglas, M. (2003). *Purity and Danger: An Analysis of Concepts of Pollution and Taboo.* New York: Routledge.

Doyle, C. with C. Wessinger & M. Wittmer. (2012). *A Journey to Waco: Autobiography of a Branch Davidian.* Lanham, MD: Rowman and Littlefield.

FBI Audiotape Q042. (1978). Transcribed by F. McGehee. *Alternative Considerations of Jonestown and Peoples Temple.* https://jonestown.sdsu .edu/?page_id=29079

Ferrara, M. S. (2019). *Communal America: Radical Experiments in Intentional Living.* New Brunswick, NJ: Rutgers University Press.

Frisk, L. (2018a). "'I Have Lived All My Life in a Reality that Doesn't Exist'. Perspectives from Ex-Members Raised in Controversial Minority Religions." In L. Frisk, S. Nilsson, & P. Åkerbäck (eds.), *Children in Minority Religions: Growing Up in Controversial Religious Groups,* 171–207. Sheffield: Equinox.

Frisk, L. (2018b). "The Waldorf Education System and Religion." In L. Frisk, S. Nilsson, & P. Åkerbäck (eds.), *Children in Minority Religions: Growing Up in Controversial Religious Groups,* 362–81. Sheffield: Equinox.

Frisk, L. (2018c). "Religion, Parenting, and Child Corporal Punishment: The Example of the Twelve Tribes." In L. Frisk, S. Nilsson, & P. Åkerbäck (eds.), *Children in Minority Religions: Growing Up in Controversial Religious Groups,* 208–30. Sheffield: Equinox.

Frisk, L. & S. Nilsson. (2021). "The Plymouth Brethren Christian Church in Sweden: Child Rearing and Schooling." *The Journal of CESNUR*, 5(2) (March–April): 135–60.

Frisk, L., S. Nilsson, & P. Åkerbäck. (2018). *Children in Minority Religions: Growing Up in Controversial Religious Groups*. Sheffield: Equinox.

Goodwin, M. (2018). "Unpacking the Bunker: Sex, Abuse, and Apocalypticism in 'Unbreakable Kimmy Schmidt'." *CrossCurrents*, 68(2) (June): 237–59. https://doi.org/10.1111/cros.12310

Greenberg, D. B. (1993). "Growing Up in Community: Children and Education within Contemporary U.S. Intentional Communities." Ph.D. diss., University of Minnesota, Minneapolis.

Grusec, J. E. & M. Davidov. (2007). "Socialization in the Family: The Roles of Parents." In J. E. Grusec & P. D. Hastings (eds.), *Handbook of Socialization: Theory and Research*, 284–303. New York: The Guilford Press.

Guest, T. (2005). *My Life in Orange: Growing Up with the Guru*. Boston, MA: Mariner Books.

Hall, J. R., P. D. Schuyler, with S. Trinh. (2000). *Apocalypse Observed: Religious Movements and Violence in North America, Europe and Japan*. London: Routledge.

Hassan, S. (1988). *Combatting Cult Mind Control*. Rochester, VT: Park Street Press.

ISKCON Child Protection Office. (2018). "History." www.iskconchildprotec tion.org/-about

ISKCON Communications. (2022). "ISKCON Imposes Ban on Bhakti Vidya Purna Swami for Sexual Abuse of Minor and Leadership Abuse." *ISKCON News*, November 14. https://iskconnews.org/iskcon-imposes-ban-on-bhakti-vidya-purna-swami-for-sexual-abuse-of-minor-and-leadership-abuse/?fbclid=IwAR2T-uewiMdwK8dWMCUd4DbLhuRnkqiHcz72Du_EEtJeTGF weaplNPb0kjM

Jenks, C. (2005). *Childhood*, 2nd ed. London: Routledge.

Lalich, J. & K. McLaren. (2018). *Escaping Utopia. Growing Up in a Cult, Getting Out and Starting Over*. New York: Routledge.

Lewis, H. S. (2005). *Oneida Lives: Long-Lost Voices of the Wisconsin Oneidas*. Lincoln: University of Nebraska Press.

Lewis, J. R. & J. A. Petersen. (2005). "Introduction." In J. R. Lewis & J. A. Petersen (eds.), *Controversial New Religions*. Oxford: Oxford University Press.

Lewis, J. R. & I. B. Tøllefsen, eds. (2016). *The Oxford Handbook of New Religious Movements*, Vol. II. New York: Oxford University Press.

Liedgren, P. (2007). "To Become, to Be and to Have Been: About the Jehovah's Witnesses." Ph.D. diss., Lund University, Lund, Sweden.

Løøv, M. (2024). *The New Age Movement*. Cambridge: Cambridge University Press.

Lutz, D. (2010). *My Karma, My Fault*. Self-published.

Melton, J. G. (2002) "The Modern Anti-Cult Movement in Historical Perspective." In Kaplan & Lööw (eds.), *The Cultic Milieu. Oppositional Subcultures in the Age of Globalization*, 265–89. Oxford: Altamira Press.

Mickler, M. (2022). *The Unification Church Movement*. Cambridge: Cambridge University Press.

Mikelsen, M. A. (1892). *The Bishop Hill Colony: A Religious Communistic Settlement in Henry County Illinois*. Baltimore, MD: Johns Hopkins Press.

Miller, M. K. (2016). "Parents' Use of Faith Healing for Their Children: Implications for the Legal System and Measuring Community Sentiment." In J. T. Richardson & F. Bellanger (eds.), *Legal Cases, New Religious Movements, and Minority Faiths*, 227–40. New York: Routledge.

Moore, R. (2006). "The Sacrament of Suicide." Was It Murder or Suicide: A Forum. *The Jonestown Report* 8. https://jonestown.sdsu.edu/?page_id=31985

Moore, R. (2022). *Peoples Temple and Jonestown in the Twenty-First Century*. Cambridge: Cambridge University Press.

Nilsson, S. (2010). "Barn i Krishna-rörelsen i Sverige: Bör vi oroa oss." *Aura: Tidskrift för akademiska studier av nyreligiositet*, 2(1): 1–21.

Nilsson, S. (2011). "Rebooting the Family: Organizational Change within the Family International." *International Journal for the Study of New Religions*, 2(2): 157–78, https://doi.org/10.1558/ijsnr.v2i2.157

Nilsson, S. (2019). "Performing Perfectly: Presentations of Childhood in Knutby Filadelfia Before and After the Dissolution of the Congregation." Ph.D. diss., Gothenburg University, Göteborg, Sweden.

Nilsson, S. (2023). *Kids of Knutby. Living In and Leaving the Swedish Filadelfia Congregation*. Cham: Switzerland: Palgrave Macmillan.

Noyes, P. (1937). *My Father's House: An Oneida Boyhood*. New York: Farrar & Rinehart.

Noyes, P. (1958). *A Goodly Heritage*. New York: Rinehart Press.

Packer, B. L. (2007). *The Transcendentalists*. Athens: University of Georgia Press.

Paden, W. E. (1994). *Religious Worlds: The Comparative Study of Religions*. Boston, MA: Beacon Press.

Palmer, S. (2004). *Aliens Adored: Räel's UFO Religion*. New Brunswick, NJ: Rutgers University Press.

Palmer, S. J. (1995). *Moon Sisters, Krishna Mothers, Rajneesh Lovers: Women's Roles in New Religions*. Syracuse, NY: Syracuse University Press.

Palmer, S. (2010). "The Twelve Tribes: Preparing the Bride for Yahshua's Return." *Nova Religio*, 13 (3): 59–80.

Palmer, S. J. (2011). "Rescuing Children? Government Raids and Child Abuse Allegations in Historical and Cross-Cultural Perspective." In S. A. Wright & J. T. Richardson (eds.), *Saints under Siege: The Texas State Raid on the Fundamentalist Latter-Day Saints*, 51–79. New York: NYU Press.

Palmer, S. J. & C. E. Hardman, eds. (1999). *Children in New Religions*. New Brunswick, NJ: Rutgers University Press.

Perry, B. & M. Szlavitz. (2006). "Stairway to Heaven: Treating Children at the Crosshairs of Trauma." ICSA e-Newsletter, 6(3), www.icsahome.com/eli brary/topics/articles/stairway-to-heaven-perry-en6-3

Pollock, L. A. (1983). *Forgotten Children: Parent-Child Relations from 1500 to 1900*. Cambridge: Cambridge University Press.

Pratezina, J. (2019). "New Religion Kids: Spiritual and Cultural Identity among Children and Youth Involved with New Religious Movements." *International Journal of Children's Spirituality*, 24(1): 73–82, https://doi.org/10.1080/1364436X.2019.1619529

Pratezina, J. (2021). "'Disciples by Default': Women's Narratives of Leaving New Religious Movements." M.A., University of Victoria, Victoria, B.C. https://dspace.library.uvic.ca/bitstream/handle/1828/12886/pratezina_jessica_MA_2021.pdf?sequence=1&isAllowed=y

Prophet, E. (2008). *Prophet's Daughter: My Life with Elizabeth Claire Prophet inside the Church Universal and Triumphant*. Guilford, CT: Lyons Press.

Puttick, E. (1999). *Women in New Religions: In Search of Community, Sexuality and Spiritual Power*. London: Palgrave Macmillan.

Richardson, J. T. (1999). "Social Control of New Religions. From 'Brainwashing' Claims to Child Sex Abuse Accusations." In Palmer & Hartman, (eds.), *Children in New Religions*, 172–86. New Brunswick, New Jersey: Rutger University Press.

Richardson, J. T., ed. (2004). *Regulating Religion: Case Studies from around the Globe*. New York: Kluwer Academic.

Richardson, J. T., J. Best, & D. G. Bromley, eds. (1991). *The Satanism Scare*. New York: Aldine de Gruyter.

Robertson, C. (1981). *Oneida Community; An Autobiography 1851–1876*. Syracuse, NY: Syracuse University Press.

Rochford, E. B. Jr. (2007). *Hare Krishna Transformed*. New York: New York University Press.

Rochford, E. B. Jr. with J. Heinlein. (1998). "Child Abuse in the Hare Krishna Movement: 1971–1986." *ISKCON Communications Journal*, 6(1) (June), https://content.iskcon.org/icj/6_1/6_1rochford.html.

Rothchild, J. & S. Wolf. (1976). *The Children of the Counterculture: How the Life-Style of America's Flower Children Has Affected an Even Younger Generation*. Garden City, NY: Doubleday.

Rother, J. (2000). *Re-member: A Handbook for Human Evolution*. Poway, CA: Lightworker.

Saliba, J. (2003). *Understanding New Religious Movements*. Walnut Creek, CA: Altamira.

Richardson, J. T. & T. L. Schreinert. (2011). "Pyrrhic Victory? An Analysis of the Appeal Court Opinions Concerning the FLDS Children." In S. A. Wright & J. T. Richardson (eds.), *Saints under Seige: The Texas State Raid on the Fundamentalist Latter-Day Saints*, 242–63. New York: New York University Press.

Schutz, A. (1967). *The Phenomenology of the Social World*. Evanston, IL: Northwestern University Press.

Schutz, A. & T. Luckmann. (1973). *The Structures of the Life World*, Vol 1. Evanston, IL: Northwestern University Press.

Shahar, S. (1990). *Childhood in the Middle Ages*. New York: Routledge.

Shorter, E. (1975). *The Making of the Modern Family*. New York: Basic Books.

Singer, M. with J. Lalich. (1995). *Cults in Our Midst*, rev. ed. San Francisco, CA: Jossey-Bass.

Singler, B. (2015). "Big Bad Pharma: The Indigo Child Concept and Biomedical Conspiracy Theories," *Nova Religion*, 19(2): 17–29.

Siskind, A. (2001). "Child-Rearing Issues in Totalistic Groups." In B. Zablocki & T. Robbins (eds.), *Misunderstanding Cults: Searching for Objectivity in a Controversial Field*, 415–51. Toronto: University of Toronto Press.

Smith, M. & L. Pazder. (1980). *Michelle Remembers*. New York: Congden and Lattés.

Sobo, E. J. & Bell, S. (2001). *Celibacy, Culture, and Society: The Anthropology of Sexual Abstinence*. Madison: University of Wisconsin Press.

Stark, R. (1996). "Why Religious Movements Succeed or Fail: A Revised General Model," *Journal of Contemporary Religion*, 11(2): 133–46, https://doi.org/10.1080/13537909608580764

Stehlik, T. (2019). *Waldorf Schools and the History of Steiner Education: An International View of 100 Years*. Cham: Switzerland: Springer International.

Stone, L. (1990). *The Family, Sex and Marriage in England 1500–1800*, abridged ed. London: Penguin Books.

Strandberg, A. (2017). *Barn & andlighet. Vägledande handbok till barn som ser, hör och känner energier från andra dimensioner*. Stockholm: Books on Demand.

Swartz, K. (2022). "Management Matters: Organizational Storytelling within the Anthroposophical Society in Sweden." Ph.D. diss., Åbo Akademi University, Turku, Finland.

Tabor, J. D. & E. V. Gallagher. (1995). *Why Waco? Cults and the Battle for Religious Freedom in America*. Berkeley: University of California Press.

Tøllefsen, I. B. & C. Giudice, eds. (2017). *Female Leaders in New Religious Movements*. London: Palgrave Macmillan.

UNICEF. (2022). Guiding Principles for Children on the Move in the Context of Climate Change. UNICEF Office of Global Insight and Policy. www.unicef.org/globalinsight/media/2796/file/UNICEF-Global-Insight-Guiding-Principles-for-children-on-the-move-in-the-context-of-climate-change-2022.pdf

Van Eck Duymaer van Twist, A. (2015). *Perfect Children: Growing Up on the Religious Fringe*. New York: Oxford University Press.

Virtue, D. (2003). *The Crystal Children: A Guide to the Newest Generation of Psychic and Sensitive Children*. London: Hay House.

Waltz, M. (2009). "From Changelings to Crystal Children: An Examination of 'New Age' Ideas about Autism." *Journal of Religion, Disability and Health*, 13(2): 114–28.

Wessinger, C. (2000). *How the Millennium Comes Violently: From Jonestown to Heaven's Gate*. New York: Seven Bridges Press.

Westbrook, D. A. (2022). *L. Ron Hubbard and Scientology Studies*. New York: Cambridge University Press.

Whedon, S. (2009). "The Wisdom of Indigo Children: An Emphatic Restatement of the Value of American Children." *Nova Religio*, 12(3): 60–76.

Wolf, D. (2004). "Child Abuse and the Hare Krishnas: History and Response." In E. F. Bryant & M. L. Ekstrand (eds.), *The Hare Krishna Movement: The Postcharismatic Fate of a Religious Transplant*, 321–44. New York: Columbia University Press.

Wooden, K. (1981). *The Children of Jonestown*. New York: McGraw-Hill.

Wright, S. A. & J. L. Fagen (2011). "6. Texas Redux: A Comparative Analysis of the FLDS and Branch Davidian Raids." In: edited by Stuart A. Wright and James T. Richardson (eds.), *Saints Under Siege: The Texas State Raid on the Fundamentalist Latter Day Saints*, 150–77. New York, USA: New York University Press. https://doi.org/10.18574/nyu/9780814795286.003.0007

Wright, S. A. & J. T. Richardson. (2011). *Saints under Siege: The Texas State Raid on the Fundamentalist Latter-Day Saints*. New York: New York University Press.

Wright, S. A. & S. J. Palmer. (2016). *Storming Zion: Government Raids on Religious Communities*. New York: Oxford University Press.

Yates, B. (2020). "Leo Ryan: How Did His Trip to Jonestown Come Together, and Why? *The Jonestown Report* 22 (October). https://jonestown.sdsu.edu/?page_id=102670

Cambridge Elements ⹀

# New Religious Movements

## Founding Editor
### †James R. Lewis
*Wuhan University*

The late James R. Lewis was a Professor of Philosophy at Wuhan University, China. He was the author or co-author of 128 articles and reference book entries, and editor or co-editor of 50 books. He was also the general editor for the *Alternative Spirituality and Religion Review* and served as the associate editor for the *Journal of Religion and Violence*. His prolific publications include *The Cambridge Companion to Religion and Terrorism* (Cambridge University Press 2017) and *Falun Gong: Spiritual Warfare and Martyrdom* (Cambridge University Press 2018).

## Series Editor
### Rebecca Moore
*San Diego State University*

Rebecca Moore is Emerita Professor of Religious Studies at San Diego State University. She has written and edited numerous books and articles on Peoples Temple and the Jonestown tragedy. Publications include *Beyond Brainwashing: Perspectives on Cultic Violence* (Cambridge University Press 2018) and *Peoples Temple and Jonestown in the Twenty-First Century* (Cambridge University Press 2022). She is reviews editor for *Nova Religio*, the quarterly journal on new and emergent religions published by the University of Pennsylvania Press.

## About the Series

Elements in New Religious Movements go beyond cult stereotypes and popular prejudices to present new religions and their adherents in a scholarly and engaging manner. Case studies of individual groups, such as Transcendental Meditation and Scientology, provide in-depth consideration of some of the most well known, and controversial, groups. Thematic examinations of women, children, science, technology, and other topics focus on specific issues unique to these groups. Historical analyses locate new religions in specific religious, social, political, and cultural contexts. These examinations demonstrate why some groups exist in tension with the wider society and why others live peaceably in the mainstream. The series highlights the differences, as well as the similarities, within this great variety of religious expressions. To discuss contributing to this series please contact Professor Moore.

Cambridge Elements ≡

# New Religious Movements

## Elements in the series

Printed in the United States
by Baker & Taylor Publisher Services